MAHATMA GANDHI

His Life and Influence

Chandra Kumar & Mohinder Puri

HEINEMANN : LONDON

William Heinemann Ltd
10 Upper Grosvenor Street, London W1X 9PA

LONDON   MELBOURNE   TORONTO
JOHANNESBURG   AUCKLAND

First published 1982
© Chandra Kumar and Mohinder Puri 1982
(cased) – 434 39865 9
(limp) – 434 39866 7

Printed and bound in Great Britain by
R J Acford Limited, Chichester

Contents

List of Illustrations

Acknowledgements

First and foremost, the authors wish to pay their own tribute to Bapu, the father of the nation, and to acknowledge the enormity of their debt to the Mahatma for giving their own lives, along with millions of their compatriots, a new sense of value and meaning. We are indebted to our publishers for providing us with an opportunity of sharing some moments from the Mahatma's experiments with truth and for reiterating Gandhiji's message of *ahimsa* and love, and would like to give our thanks in particular to Nigel Hollis and Caroline Ball for their advice and assistance in the preparation of this tribute.

It is no easy task to capture and project the rich, diverse and long life of the Mahatma, spanning three-quarters of a century. We are grateful to the authors of numerous works on Gandhi for according us permission to reproduce extracts from their books: to The Bodley Head and David Higham Associates Ltd for *The Life and Death of Mahatma Gandhi* by Robert Payne; Oxford University Press, New Delhi for *Mahatma Gandhi, A Biography* by B. R. Nanda; William Heinemann Ltd for *Gandhi: A Study in Revolution* by Geoffrey Ashe, reprinted by permission of A. D. Peters & Co Ltd; Odhams Press Ltd for *Mahatma Gandhi* by H. S. Polak, H. N. Brailsford and Lord Pethick-Lawrence; Cambridge University Press for *Gandhi's Rise to Power* by Judith M. Brown and *Gandhi* by F. W. Rawding; Asia Publishing House for *Gandhi Through Western Eyes* by Horace Alexander; George Allen & Unwin Ltd for *Mahatma Gandhi: Essays and Reflections,* edited by Dr S. Radhakrishnan; Heinemann Educational Books for *Political Values and the Educated Class in Africa* by Ali A. Mazrui; Johnson Publishing Co. for *What Manner of Man* by Lerone Bennet Jr.; and Sphere Books for *Kaunda on Violence* by Kenneth David Kaunda, edited by Colin M. Morris © Kenneth David Kaunda 1980, published by Sphere Books Ltd 1982.

It is not possible to write about Gandhiji without quoting from his own writings and we offer our sincere thanks to Navajivan Publishing House, Ahmedabad, that unique institution which has performed remarkable service in the dissemination of Gandhi's example and message to India and the world. Mr Pyare Lal, formerly editor of *Harijan,* Mahatma's secretary and dedicated biographer, expressed his candid views on Gandhi's relevance to today's world during an interview with Mohinder Puri when he called upon him during our research for this book. We are also grateful to him for allowing us to quote from his books on Gandhi.

We also wish to convey our sincere thanks to Shri Vithalbhai Jhaveri (co-editor with Mr Tendulkar of the celebrated eight-volume biography of Gandhi and producer of the film *Mahatma*) for his generous offer to Mohinder Puri, when he met him at Mani Bhavan in Bombay, to reproduce some of the historical photographs relating to Gandhi's life from one of the finest collections in India, the Sumati Morarjee Collection. We are also fortunate in enjoying the close cooperation of the Ministry of Information and Broadcasting of the Government of India. Mr S. B. Lal, the Secretary of the Ministry gave us invaluable advice in our search for photographs and copyright material. Our thanks are also due to Mr Ahmed, Director of the Gandhi museum in Delhi for making available a representative collection of the Mahatma's photographs for our use. Our special thanks also go to Mr Khushwant Singh, Chief Editor of the *Hindustan Times,* New Delhi, who readily gave us access and permission to use photographs from the *Hindustan Times* photograph library. Amongst several other friends who assisted us in India, we would like to make special mention of Mrs Usha S Mehta for her valuable help.

London and other centres in Great Britain have splendid collections of Gandhian literature and photographs and we received generous assistance from many organisations, libraries and peace movements. We would like to thank many erstwhile colleagues of Chandra Kumar at the Commonwealth Institute, London: Fred Lightfoot, Deputy Director, for his warm support and encouragement; John Callender, Chief Education Officer and Moses J. Ntuk–Idem of the Education Department and Ronald Warwick for their advice. Our thanks also go to Dr Bingle of the India Office Library and Records (now a part of the British Library), librarians and staffs of India House, the Royal Commonwealth Society, the Royal Institute of International Affairs and the University of London (S.O.A.S.). Our grateful thanks also go to India House, London, for allowing us to use some excellent photographs from their collection. We were also able to profit from the advice and guidance of prominent Gandhians in Great Britain: Shri Devi Prasad, who was closely associated with Gandhi and Tagore in constructive programmes, and an active worker with the peace movement and War Resisters International; Mr Dharam Pal, a close associate of Mirabehn and Satish Kumar, Vinoba Bhave's disciple and a sarvodaya worker. Chandra Kumar would also like to express his appreciation for the advice of his son, Pradeep, a social worker in London and a devoted follower of Gandhi, who is active in the promotion of village self-help projects in India and was of great help in the interpretation of Gandhi's appeal to the younger generation.

Preface

MOHANDAS KARAMCHAND GANDHI'S life is the unique story of an average individual, shy, self-conscious, subject to all the human frailties, who rose by dedicated effort, love and an abiding faith in humanity to become one of the greatest leaders of India and the world in modern times. This metamorphosis of an ordinary person into a Mahatma, a Great Soul, is an inspiring example for all generations, and a vivid demonstration of what can be accomplished by determination, discipline and "right conduct". It is difficult to understand the history of the first half of our century without understanding the part played by Gandhi in liberating India and in expediting the retreat of British and European imperialism. Gandhi does not belong to India alone. Louis Fischer, his renowned American biographer, has described him as India's gift to the modern world.

Gandhi's life and thoughts are well documented: over 400 books, biographies, studies and analyses, commentaries, anthologies and bibliographies have been published in several languages. The Mahatma's autobiography, *My Experiments with Truth*, contains his own observations and version of the impact that persons and events made on him during the first 50 years of his life. The story of his last 25 years, which he lived constantly in the public eye, was recorded in the weekly journals *Young India* and *Harijan*, through his speeches and voluminous correspondence, and by dedicated biographers. His secretary, Pyare Lal, has given us in *Early Phase* and *Last Phase* two great works of remarkable insight, and Tendulkar and Jhaveri's *Mahatma* in eight profusely illustrated volumes, reveals a unique understanding of the diverse strands of Gandhi's life and thoughts and contains a wealth of detail. In addition, every word that the Mahatma spoke and wrote has been recorded in a monumental publication: *The Collected Works of Mahatma Gandhi* which runs to over 85 volumes, each containing about 550 pages. There are several other excellent studies of Gandhi's life and teachings in the English language, besides books in several foreign languages and India's regional languages.

This book provides a brief introduction to the life of Mahatma Gandhi and its significance for our present-day world. Gandhi is a living presence in India and his message of truth and non-violence still wields considerable influence in many other countries, associations, organizations and protest movements. Several books and studies on Gandhi appeared between 1968 and 1969, on the occasion of the Gandhi centenary celebrations, and his teachings still bear great relevance in today's world and will continue to do so for many years. By highlighting the salient events from the Mahatma's life and bringing the story of his impact in India and the world up to date, we hope to give an insight into the true character of the man, and through the various extracts from his writings provide a greater appreciation of his humanity and wisdom.

Chandra Kumar
Mohinder Puri

Chapter 1
—⋄ Early Life ⋄—

PERCHED ON THE west coast of India, on the outer fringe of the peninsula of Kathiawar, jutting out into the Arabian Sea, lies the city of Porbandar. Its harbour had for centuries been a spring-board for Gujarati adventurers, traders and seamen who had taken off in their various vessels for distant outposts in the Arabian peninsula, the Middle East and the Eastern seaboard of Africa. In the nineteenth century Kathiawar, now a part of Gujarat state, was fragmented into over two hundred tiny states, principalities and fiefs, each with its own ruler or overlord. These native states, here and elsewhere in India, were not directly administered by the British Government, but they nevertheless enjoyed imperial protection. British agents and advisers kept a close watch on their affairs and exercised remote or direct control as the situation demanded.

Porbandar was one of these small semi-autonomous states, with a population of a little over 72,000 and a ruler, entitled to an eleven-gun salute, who lived in his palace in the town, next to the harbour. The lanes in the town were narrow and winding, the bazaars crowded and treeless, but although the buildings were not very impressive, the temples not outstanding specimens of architecture, the town had a dream-like air about it. This, surprisingly enough, was imparted by the soft, white stone from the local quarries which had been used in the construction of Porbandar and its encompassing walls. These massive stone walls, almost twenty feet thick, stood as sentinels around the small town as protection from the fury of the waves which would mercilessly lash and pound the coast, and as a bulwark against marauders from across the sea. With the passage of time and exposure to the elements, the stone had acquired a rock-like impregnability and the soft hue of pure white marble, which sparkled in the sun and glowed when bathed in moonlight, giving Porbandar the name of The White City.

In this "White City", on 2nd October 1869, a son was born to Putlibai, wife of Karamchand Uttamchand Gandhi, the *Diwan*, or prime minister, of the tiny state of Porbandar. It was twelve years after the "Revolt" otherwise described as The Indian Sepoy Mutiny, and a little over eight years before Queen Victoria assumed the title of Empress of India. 2nd October was an ordinary day like any other and was not marked by any other event of great significance or unusual conjunction of heavenly bodies, and no one could have guessed that the infant Gandhi, with his long ears, large eyes and captivating smile, born in Porbandar on this day, would have a monumental impact on the course of history in the first half of the twentieth century.

Mohandas Karamchand was the third son born to Karamchand and Putlibai in the large three-storey ancestral house which had belonged to the Gandhi family for three generations. Karamchand Gandhi lived in this house with his five brothers, and it was here that Mohandas, along with his two brothers, a sister, and various cousins and uncles and aunts grew up. The Gandhis, who were originally grocers, belonged to the *Modh Bania* sub-caste of *Vaishyas*, who rank third in the hierarchical caste structure of Hindu society.

It may be recalled that the caste system was evolved out of the four social divisions, based on occupations: *Brahmins* (priests and scholars), *Kshatriyas* (nobles and warriors), *Vaishyas* (farmers and merchants) and *Shudras* (workers). In course of time, these divisions became stratified and split into many sub-castes and the *Banias* have a reputation in India for being astute and clever businessmen.

The Gandhi family had relinquished their traditional occupations and exhibited a flair for administrative work and an acumen for political manoeuvres and strategem. Mohandas's grandfather Uttamchand had risen to fame as a high calibre administrator and the ruler of Porbandar had appointed him as prime minister of the state. The *Diwans* were appointed by the rulers, rather than by election, and therefore generally came from families with close connections or family ties to the ruler himself, but it required considerable tact and diplomatic skill to steer safely between the whims and caprices of autocratic rulers and the British political agents, who could often prove arrogant and temperamental. Uttamchand had changed masters many times, and had been prime minister of several states; he must have been a very remarkable man indeed. Writing about him in his autobiography, many years later, Gandhi recorded:

> My grandfather must have been a man of principle. State intrigues compelled him to leave Porbandar, where he was *Diwan* and to seek refuge in Junagadh. There he saluted the *Nawab* [ruler] with the left hand. Someone noticing the apparent discourtesy asked for an explanation, and Uttamchand replied, "The right hand is already pledged to Porbandar."

Mohandas's father, Karamchand, was a man of little education but was blessed with qualities of head and heart that won him a name, reputation and many friends and admirers. Gandhi, writing about his father in his autobiography, said:

> My father was a lover of his clan, truthful, brave and generous. To a certain extent he might have been given to carnal pleasures, for he married for the fourth time when he was over forty. But he was incorruptible and had earned a name for strict impartiality in his family as well as outside. He had no education, save that of experience. . . . Of history and geography, he was innocent. But his rich practical experience stood him in good stead in the solution of most intricate questions and in managing hundreds of men.

A gulf of 50 years divided the father and the son. Mohandas, when he grew up, held his father in great reverence and awe although as the youngest son became more attached to his mother. In assessing the influence of the parents on the child, the influ-

1   Gandhi's mother, Putlibai

ence of his father is often not fully appreciated. Robert Payne in his book *The Life and Death of Mahatma Gandhi*★ observes:

> In later years the son [Mohandas] would say that he derived most of his character from his mother, but this was to underestimate the influence of the father. A surviving photograph of Karamchand shows a sensitive face with regular features, a straight nose, small eyes, a firm and slightly jutting chin, and a heavy handlebar moustache. He gazes out of the photograph with a quiet air of authority, and he was clearly a man who pondered very carefully before coming to decisions. He had not the least resemblance to his youngest son, who evidently took after his mother.

Mohandas, affectionately known in the family as Mohania or just Mohan, grew up at Porbandar amidst his large family of uncles, aunts, cousins, an affectionate if somewhat stern father, and a doting mother. As the youngest in the family, he was no doubt pampered and was allowed to have things his own way, and as the son of the *Diwan* of Porbandar, he was treated with considerable deference. But he was a rather shy and somewhat timid child, scared of ghosts and darkness. At the age of three, he had a nurse called Rambha to whom he became very attached. Mohan took her into his confidence and confessed that he was frightened of ghosts. She assured him that there were no ghosts, but if he was afraid, he could repeat the name of Rama, the Hindu god who was a re-incarnation of Vishnu. All his life Mohan did not forget this early advice and the last words uttered by him when he was assassinated was *He Rama* (Oh Rama).

But it was his mother's example and devotion which was to be Gandhi's chief influence in his formative years.

Putlibai was a noble, gracious lady and a living picture of love and self-sacrifice. She was also highly religious and somehow managed to divide her day admirably between the home and the temple. Mohan was the youngest member of the family, and she undoubtedly indulged him to excess, but he was devoted to her, and his mother's abounding maternal love and her saintliness made a deep impression upon him; he imbibed some of her qualities of love and sacrifice and a passion for nursing. Gandhi wrote later:

> The outstanding impression my mother left on my memory is that of saintliness. She was deeply religious. She would not think of taking her meals without her daily prayers. . . . She would take the hardest vows and keep them without flinching. Illness was no excuse for relaxing them. To keep two or three consecutive fasts was nothing to her. Living on one meal a day during *Chaturmas* [a period of fasting and semi-fasting during the four months of the rains – a sort of long Lent period] was a habit with her.

Gandhi continued:

> Once during another *Chaturmas* she vowed not to have food without seeing the sun. We children on those days would stand, staring at the sky, waiting to announce the appearance of the sun to our mother. Everyone knows that at the height of the rainy season the sun often does not condescend to show its face. And I remember days when at its sudden ap-

★ The Bodley Head, London, 1969

pearance we would rush and announce it to her. She would run out to see with her own eyes, but by that time the fugitive sun would be gone, thus depriving her of her meal. "That does not matter," she would say cheerfully, "God did not want me to eat today." And then she would return to her round of duties.

Mohandas had no formal schooling until he was seven, but he seems to have attended a private school where children were taught to write the letters of the Gujarati alphabet in the dust. About this school he wrote in his autobiography:

I recollect having been put to school. It was with some difficulty that I got through multiplication tables. The fact that I recollect nothing more of those days than having learnt, in company with other boys, to call our teachers all kinds of names, would strongly suggest that my intellect must have been sluggish and my memory raw.

He was not, however, above mischief or boyish pranks, although his high regard for truth and honesty already acquired from his parents would not allow him to lie about his misdeeds.

One day he and his clan of cousins decided to raid the local temples of the god Vishnu and his consort Lakshami and collect the bronze images of the gods and goddesses, while the temple priest was indulging in a siesta. Unfortunately for them, one of the images fell down with a loud clang and the priest, who woke up on hearing this sound, gave chase. The gang was caught red-handed. During cross-examination all children save Mohan denied that they had anything to do with the theft. Mohan, then six, was the only one to come out with the truth.

When Mohan was seven years old, his father Karamchand was appointed *Diwan* of Rajkot, one of the peninsula's small inland states. It had better schooling facilities

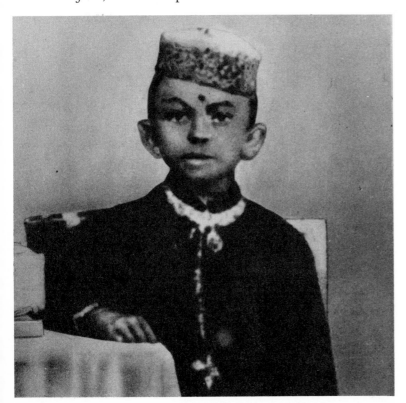

2 Mohandas Gandhi at the age of seven

3 The primary school at Rajkot which Gandhi attended

than Porbandar and Mohan's education was begun in all seriousness. In his own words Gandhi later stated:

> As at Porbandar, so here at Rajkot, there is hardly anything to note about my studies. I could only have been a mediocre student. From this school, I went to the suburban school and thence to the high school having reached my twelfth year.

Mohan was a shy and self-conscious boy and he himself comments on this trait and its implications:

> I used to be very shy and avoided all company. My books and my lessons were my sole companions. To be at the school at the stroke of the hour and to run back home as soon as the school closed – that was my daily habit, because I could not bear to talk to anybody. I was even afraid, lest anyone should poke fun at me.

Child marriages did not seem to be the practice in ancient India, but appear to have become popular in the north and the western regions amongst the Hindus during the middle ages. This trend, which had probably arisen during the periods of insecurity and instability as a result of foreign invasions, was in vogue in Kathiawar during the nineteenth century. Marriage amongst Hindus is a very elaborate and costly affair; parents abandon all financial restraints during these occasions and the lavish expense leads in many cases to financial ruin. Preparations start months ahead with the making of expensive clothes and jewellery, a large variety of sweets and courses are got ready, and no expense is spared in trying to outdo others.

Mohan was thirteen when preparations for his wedding to Kasturbai, also thirteen, were afoot. The bride's father Seth Gokuldas Makanji lived not very far from the Gandhi family in Porbandar and Mohan had been engaged to Kasturbai at the age of seven but he remembered little about it except that Kasturbai had no education and was small for her age. In order to save money, it had been decided that Mohan's elder brother, a year or two older, and a cousin should also be married at the same time in a triple wedding. Writing with hindsight in his autobiography, Gandhi denounces the "cruel system of child marriage" but at the time it was all fun and excitement, and recalling it more than 40 years later, he remembered all the details:

> I do not think it meant to me anything more than the prospect of good clothes to wear, drum beating, marriage processions, rich dinners and a strange girl to play with. The carnal desire came later.

Karamchand sustained injuries during his journey by coach from Rajkot to Porbandar and arrived covered in bandages, but the marriages were not postponed. Times and dates for weddings selected by the priests are considered auspicious and it is not easy to change them. Gandhi continues his account:

> My father put on a brave face in spite of his injuries and took full part in the wedding. . . . Little did I realize that one day I would severely criticize him for having married me off as a child. Everything on that day seemed to be right and proper and pleasing. There was also my eagerness to get married . . . I can picture to myself, even today, how we sat on our wedding dais, how we performed the *Satapadi* [seven steps], how we, the newly wedded husband and wife put the sweet *Kansar* [a preparation of wheat] into each other's mouth and how we began to live together. . . .

Talking about the wedding night he continues:

> Two innocent children all unwittingly hurled themselves into the ocean of life. My brother's wife had thoroughly coached me about my behaviour on the first night. I do not know who had coached my wife. . . . But no coaching is really necessary in such matters. The impressions of the former birth are potent enough to make all coaching superfluous. We gradually began to know each other, and to speak freely together. We were the same age. But I took no time in assuming the authority of a husband.

The western reader may be somewhat baffled or intrigued by some of the assumptions or observations in the above quote from Gandhi's autobiography. Gandhi's marriage to Kasturbai was an arranged marriage and it lasted 62 years. The reference to "former birth" is based on the Hindu belief in the cycle of births and deaths, and the transmigration of souls. This belief lends itself to the romantic assumption that you and your life-partner in this life, have been or would be life companions in earlier or future lives. Suspension of disbelief in such explanations about life and death can only be made in the inner recesses of the mind and can not be analysed or dissected in scientific laboratories.

The "cruel system" of early marriage could only be sustained in the traditional joint family system where grandparents, parents, children and sons' wives and children all lived under one roof. The newly-weds in the Gandhi family did not have to worry about finding a job, home and furnishings, furniture and household equipment. The harshness of the early marriage custom was also mitigated to some extent by the enforced separation of the couples for long periods as a result of young brides having to go back to their parents' homes for fairly long periods every year, especially during the earlier years of the marriage.

The teenage husbands, Mohandas and his brother Karsandas, were both expected to go back to school and resume their interrupted studies. Both lost a year at school and his brother gave up studies altogether, but Mohandas was being prompted to pay more attention to his studies in the hope that some day he might step into his father's shoes as *Diwan*. The prospect of assuming family responsibilities one day made him work harder but the thoughts of his wife and the prospect of meeting her each night continually haunted Mohan; and we learn more about the dilemma in his own words:

> I must say, I was passionately fond of her, and the thought of nightfall and our subsequent meeting was ever haunting me. I used to keep her awake with my idle talk. If with this devouring passion, there had not been in me a burning attachment to duty, I should have either fallen a prey to disease and premature death or have sunk into a burdensome existence. But the appointed tasks had to be gone through every morning and lying to anyone was out of the question. It was this last thing which saved me from many a pitfall.

Gandhi continued his studies, with only modest success, but his adolescent years provided him with lessons that were to develop or reinforce the moral principles instilled in him from early childhood.

Like most young Indians, he was familiar with the legendary Hindu heroes. The stories of Shravana and Rama, so often cited as examples of filial duty or moral rectitude, made a deep impression on Mohandas, and a theatrical version of a story about King Harishchandra who gives up his wife and all he owns and suffers extreme privation for the sake of the vindication of truth, moved Mohan as nothing else had. The ideals of absolute truth and absolute duty were firmly impressed on his mind despite temptations from the world outside the influence of his family.

Mehtab, an extrovert young Muslim friend, once confided that he was not afraid of ghosts or snakes and that his fearlessness was due to the eating of meat. He quoted the popular doggerel ascribed to a Gujarati poet:

> Behold the Mighty Englishman,
> He rules the Indian small,
> Because being a meat eater,
> He is five cubits tall,
> A host to himself,
> A match for five hundred.

Meat eating and smoking were forbidden to members of the *Vaishanava* community, but Mohan did wish to grow taller, stronger and have more courage, and agreed

4   Alfred High School, Rajkot

to try meat on the quiet, as he did not wish to antagonize and pain his parents. After a few furtive experiments, however, he had to confess that his conscience would not allow such a deception and he had reluctantly to forgo the promise of increased height and courage, bringing an end to his meat-eating aspirations.

It was Mehtab also, who took Mohan to a brothel and Gandhi, several years later, recalled what happened:

> He sent me in with the necessary instructions. It was all pre-arranged. The bill had already been paid. God, in his infinite mercy, protected me against myself. I was almost struck dumb in this den of vice. I sat near the woman on her bed, but I was tongue-tied. She naturally lost patience with me and showed me the door.

When, in 1894, Gandhi was a leading lawyer with a flourishing practice in South Africa he had not forgotten his schoolmate, Mehtab, who had not been doing so well in life, and invited him to come and stay in his large and comfortable house in Natal. He wanted to help him and no doubt use his influence to reform Mehtab. Old habits die hard, however, and one day his irrepressible old school friend was caught red-handed with the prostitutes he invited to the house while Gandhi was away at the office. Gandhi was full of rage at this disgraceful conduct and asked Mehtab to leave his house immediately. Subsequently, it is understood, Mehtab did change his ways, got married and his wife and daughter became satyagrahis; by this time Gandhi had forgiven him.

5   Karamchand Uttamchand Gandhi, *Diwan* of Porbandar

Smoking was another taboo and he, along with his accomplices, went through the stages of all adolescent schoolboys embarking on this surreptitious route. They started by smoking cigarette ends and stole coppers from a domestic servant's pittance of pocket money to buy cigarettes. In the event they were overcome with a sense of remorse and guilt over this secret vice and decided upon a suicide pact in a temple. At the last moment, they could not summon enough courage to administer the lethal poison and decided to forget it all as a bad joke. Writing about this silly experiment later, he wrote: "Ever since I have grown up, I have never desired to smoke and have always regarded the habit of smoking as barbarous."

A moving episode, which was the result of his temporary smoking escapades is described in his own words: "I pilfered the coppers when I was twelve or thirteen, possibly less. The other theft was committed when I was fifteen. In this case, I stole a bit of gold out of my meat-eating brother's armlet." This brother, had run into a debt of some twenty-five rupees and Mohan cleared the debt with the small "bit" and he decided never to steal again. He had not however bargained with his conscience, which prompted him to confess his guilt to his father, since "there could not be a cleansing without a clean confession." He decided to write out his confession to submit it to his father and ask for his forgiveness. Gandhi writes:

> I was trembling as I handed the confession to my father. I handed him the note and sat opposite. . . . He read it through, and pearl-drops trickled down the cheeks, wetting the paper. For a moment he closed his eyes in thought and then tore up the note . . . I also cried. I could see my father's agony. . . . Those pearl-drops of love cleansed my heart, and washed my sin away. Only he who had experienced such love can know what it is. As the hymn says:

> "Only he,
> Who is smitten with the arrows of love,
> Knows its power."

When Mohandas was in his sixteenth year, his father was bed-ridden, suffering from a fistula. Mohan, his mother and an old servant of the house attended Karamchand and every night Mohan massaged his father's legs. His wife was expecting a baby but he did not find it easy to restrain his carnal desires even in this state of affairs. His father's health was deteriorating day by day. One evening about 10.30 or 11 p.m., when he was giving the massage, his uncle offered to relieve him and Mohan darted for the bedroom and started making love to his wife. Little did he realize that his father was passing through his last moments of life. Within five or six minutes, there was a knock on the door and he was informed, "Father is no more."

This was a traumatic moment in Mohandas's life. He was never able to forgive himself for his shame, the shame of his carnal desire at the critical hour of his father's death. Describing this shame in his autobiography, he recorded:

> So all was over. I had but to wring my hands. I felt deeply ashamed and miserable . . . I felt that, if animal passion had not blinded me, I should have been spared the torture of separation from my father during his last moments.

Mohan scraped through the Matriculation examination without gaining distinction in any subject, and joined Samaldas College in Bhavnagar, some ninety miles away from Rajkot, for his B.A. Somehow, he could not progress with his studies. He writes:

> [I] found myself entirely at sea. Everything was difficult. I could not follow, let alone take an interest in the professors' lectures. It was no fault of theirs. The professors in that College were regarded as first-rate. But I was so raw. At the end of the first term, I returned home.

At this time an old friend and adviser of the family suggested to his mother and elder brother that instead of letting Mohan pursue his college studies at Bhavnagar, it would be more advantageous to send him to England for three years to qualify as a barrister. With a foreign legal qualification, Mohandas would have a better chance and claim to the *Diwan*ship of Porbandar or Rajkot, or to settle down to a lucrative legal practice. Mohan welcomed the suggestion and expressed his keenness to go to England.

There were some hurdles to be crossed. With the passing away of the father, the family was not very well off financially and the amount required for expenses on the passage and three years' stay in London, would have to be raised by loans. Secondly, orthodox sections of the Hindu society did not welcome the idea of young men going overseas to England and falling prey to the temptations of drink and sex and non-vegetarian food. Young Gandhi was however determined to go and once the money had been arranged, the other difficulty was overcome by his taking solemn vows before his mother to abstain from wine, women and meat. Once the vows had been administered and undertaken in all solemnity, his mother gave him permission to proceed to England, leaving behind his wife and child.

Chapter 2
In the Land of Philosophers and Poets:
—◦❧ London Years and After ❦◦—

IT WAS SEPTEMBER 1888, and Mohandas, the shy and diffident boy from Rajkot, had shown remarkable powers of persistence in overcoming all opposition in his path. He was not quite nineteen, yet once he had set his heart on going to England, "the land of philosophers and poets" as he called it, nothing could have deflected him from pursuing his goal. The waiting period in Bombay before departure had seemed to drag on much too long for comfort, and as he was about to sail, the *Modh Bania* caste community in Bombay had become agitated about his going abroad. Mohan was summoned before the "caste tribunal" and told by the *Sheth* – the headman of the community – that his proposed trip to England would compromise Hindu religion, because he would be obliged to eat and drink with Europeans. Mohan however, had not been overawed and defied their injunction to him to cancel the trip. The tribunal excommunicated him from the community, but Mohandas did not show any concern about being branded an outcaste; it only heightened his anxiety to escape.

Finally, on 4th September, he was able to leave all his tribulations behind and set sail aboard S.S. *Clyde*, to distant lands and unfamiliar places. His only acquaintance on the ship was a Mr Mazumdar, a lawyer and "an experienced man of mature age", who shared his second class cabin. The cosmopolitan atmosphere on the ship was in marked contrast with life in Porbandar and Rajkot. Mohan had only a nodding acquaintance with the English language and was quite unaccustomed to talking in the language. He says in his journal:

> I had to frame every sentence in my mind, before I could bring it out. I was innocent of the use of knives and forks and had not the boldness to inquire what dishes on the menu were free of meat. I therefore never took meals at table but always had them in my cabin and they consisted principally of fruits and sweets, which I had brought with me.

In the beginning, he confined himself to his cabin most of the time, but gradually he acquired a little courage and exchanged a few sentences with friendly fellow passengers.

Well-meaning passengers argued that it would not be possible for Mohan to survive in the cold climate of England without eating meat. At this stage he was a vegetarian through family upbringing, and not because of any conviction that it was the right thing to do. What mattered more than anything else to him, was the fact that he had taken a vow before his mother that he would not touch meat or wine. His very high regard for his mother, an unusual passion for honesty and truth and a very strong will-power to back up his vows and promises meant more to him than the tradition itself. He was prepared to go back to India rather than break a solemn vow. In the event he survived the rigours of the journey on a vegetarian diet, and reached London on 27th October.

As he stepped out, he was wearing a white flannel suit, the only person wearing summer clothes in what was already winter. He had brought with him four letters of introduction: Dr P. J. Mehta, a friend of the Gandhis, Prince Ranjitsinghji, the renowned cricketer, Mr D. Shukla, and Dadabhai Naoroji, one of the most distinguished Indians in Britain, who later became Member of Parliament for Finsbury. Mohan and Mazumdar found rooms in the Victoria Hotel, an ornate but rather expensive hotel on Northumberland Avenue, near Trafalgar Square. Dr Mehta called on Mohandas at the Victoria the same evening, wearing a top hat. Mohan liked the texture of the hat and passed his hand over it, the wrong way about, without the permission of the owner. Dr Mehta was not amused and gave young Gandhi his first lessons in European etiquette. He also advised Mohandas to find accommodation with a landlady. Hotels were far too expensive.

His first days in London were far from happy. He was terribly lonely in an alien environment with a different approach to life and felt like an exile from his country, his people and his home. It was a transitional stage and the nostalgia that he had for his home and family at the time was not substantially different in nature from that which afflicted almost all Indian students who found themselves transplanted to an unfamiliar environment, far removed from the love and companionship found in large or joint families. Gandhi recalls very vividly his thoughts and yearnings in those days:

> I would continually think of my home and my country. My mother's love always haunted me. At night the tears would stream down my cheeks, and home memories of all sorts made sleep out of the question. . . . Everything was strange, the people, their ways and even their dwellings.

The sacred vow to remain a teetotaller and a vegetarian was an embarrassment and not conducive to the formation of friendships, or so it seemed anyway at that time. He continues:

> There was the additional inconvenience of the vegetarian vow. Even the dishes that I could eat were tasteless and insipid. I thus found myself between Scylla and Charybdis. England I could not bear, but to return to India was not to be thought of. Now that I had come, I must finish the three years, said the inner voice.

He listened to his "inner voice" and enrolled himself for the Bar at the Inner Temple, where he took to his studies seriously, involving himself in the study of Roman law and Common law, and scrupulously studying the prescribed textbooks, rather than cramming himself with information derived from notes as a short-cut to success.

The other requirement was "keeping terms" and this meant attendance at a prescribed number of dinners each term. His enrolment at the Middle Temple meant he had to apply himself zealously to the improvement of his standard of proficiency in the English language and on the advice of a friend he started reading newspapers, poring over *The Daily News, The Daily Telegraph* and the *Pall Mall Gazette*. In the course of time, he acquired considerable facility and ease in scanning the newspapers and the daily dose became a life-time habit. At the same time he also decided to appear for the Matriculation examination of London University as a private candidate. Mohandas's life was becoming more meaningful and crowded, and there was hardly time for brooding over loneliness.

And then, during this period, he decided that the vow of vegetarianism need not inhibit him from acquiring other graces and refinements. He decided to become An English Gentleman. He bought a new outfit of clothes from the Army and Navy Stores and spent the generous sum of ten pounds on an evening dress suit made in Bond Street. He also bought a top hat or the so-called "Chimney-pot" hat, similar to the one that Dr Mehta had sported in the Victoria Hotel. To complete the ensemble, brother Laxmidas's help was also sought. "I got my good and noble-hearted brother to send me a double watch-chain of gold." He grappled successfully with the art of tying a tie and grooming his hair.

A friend who came across Mohandas in Piccadilly some time in 1890 has left a vivid and amusing pen-picture of his sartorial elegance:

> He was wearing a high silk top hat, polished bright, a stiff starched collar, a flashy tie of all the colours of the rainbow under which was a fine-striped silk shirt. He wore a morning coat, a double-breasted waist-coat and dark striped trousers. He had leather gloves and a silver topped cane and was at the very height of fashion for a young man about town.

6   The English Gentleman: Gandhi as a law student in London

He also paid attention to the other accomplishments required of a gentleman. Mohan decided to take lessons in dancing and paid the princely sum of £3 for a term's lessons but discovered after a matter of five or six that "it was beyond me to achieve anything like rhythmic motion. I could not follow the piano and hence found it impossible to keep time." Undaunted, he embarked upon violin lessons – investing £3 in an instrument, plus fees – and elocution lessons, beginning with a speech of Pitt's in Bell's *Standard Elocution*.

In all, his efforts in acquiring the polish of a gentleman lasted approximately three months, and no more than two or three lessons in elocution, before he punned "Mr Bell rang the bell of alarm in my ear and I awoke." He realized that it was his character that would make a gentleman out of him rather than the external attributes that he had been trying to cultivate, and devoted himself to his studies, the main purpose of his visit to England.

Mohandas now turned a new leaf and the aspirant English gentleman became a serious student. While the Bar examinations did not require much study, the syllabus of the London Matriculation course included Latin and another modern language and was a formidable challenge. He realized that study of Latin, however difficult, would prove useful in understanding law books. Apart from the fact that the paper on Roman law was entirely in Latin, knowledge of this language would also give him greater command over the English language and in spite of initial difficulties, he acquired a taste for Latin and studied French as the modern language.

Mohandas also came to realize that his way of living was beyond the modest means of his family. He decided to make a drastic cut in his expenses and to change his lifestyle by taking rooms on his own and cooking his own meals instead of living with a family. He moved from place to place in closer proximity to his place of business or work. He could thereby cut down his bus fares and other expenses. This also gave him the opportunity and the leisure time for long walks of eight or ten miles a day. This habit of walking was not only useful to him for maintaining good health throughout his stay, but it was the best way of getting to know the city. By 1890, he had gathered so much information about London that he had enough confidence to compile a guide to London for Indian students of modest means and similar tastes and interests so that they could profit by his trials, errors and experiences in the discovery of London.

His main cause for anxiety and concern seemed to be food, and his vow to abstain from meat not only led him into awkward and embarrassing situations but the paucity of vegetarian food kept him at a level of semi-starvation most of the time. One day, however, he was in luck. During one of his long walks in London, he stumbled upon a vegetarian restaurant in Farringdon Street, in the heart of London. His joy knew no bounds – he walked in and had his first big meal since leaving the shores of India. He also bought a book, *A Plea for Vegetarianism* by Henry Salt. The book impressed him and during the next few weeks, he devoured whatever other literature he could lay his hands on, including *The Perfect Way in Diet* by Dr Anna Kingsford and the Howard Williams' *Ethics of Diet* . These books revolutionized his life, and

7　The London Vegetarian Society of which Gandhi (*front right*) was a member of the Executive Committee

for the first time, his sentimental attachment to vegetarianism became a matter of conviction.

Mohandas's reasoned conversion to vegetarianism transformed the tempo of life in London. He became a member of the Vegetarian Society and a dedicated worker for the movement. He came out of his shell and found he could enter British society through another channel. He started writing for *The Vegetarian* and contributed nine articles on the dietary habits of Indians and their social life and customs. These articles were highly appreciated by the members and he was elected to the executive committee of the Society. Describing his enthusiasm for the cause, he says:

> A convert's enthusiasm for his new religion is greater than that of a person born in it. Vegetarianism was then a new cult in England. . . . Full of the neophyte's zeal for vegetarianism, I decided to start a vegetarian club in my locality, Bayswater. I invited Sir Edwin Arnold, who lived there, to be Vice-President. Dr Oldfield, who was the editor of *The Vegetarian* became President. I myself became the Secretary.

B. R. Nanda, states in his biography of Gandhi:

> The discovery of this restaurant [the vegetarian restaurant in Farringdon Street] was an event more significant than he could see at the moment. There was a long and hard but

sure road which led from Farringdon Street in London to the Phoenix and Tolstoy Settlements in South Africa, and to the Sabarmati and Sevagram Ashrams in India.★

From vegetarianism to religion and philosophy was an easy transition, especially as Sir Edwin Arnold was, as well as an eminent vegetarian, the author of *The Light of Asia*, the immortal poem on the life of Gautama the Buddha, and *The Song Celestial*, the English translation of the divine poem *Bhagvad Gita*, the holy book of the Hindus. It is held in the same kind of reverence in Hinduism, as the Koran in Islam, the Old Testament in Judaism and the New Testament in Christianity. Mohandas had not read *Gita* in Sanskrit and his first introduction to it was through Edwin Arnold's inspired translation. Later on, however, he read the original poem in Sanskrit and many other translations and finally he translated it into Gujarati himself. The teachings of *Bhagvad Gita* had a profound influence on Gandhi and he tried all his life to live and practise the message of the *Gita*, the divine song.

One thing led to another and the reading of *The Song Celestial* was followed by a study of the Bible; he was deeply moved by the Sermon on the Mount. From Christ he moved to the life of Prophet Mohammed. In the chapter on the Hero as a prophet, in Thomas Carlyle's *Heroes and Hero-Worship*, he "learnt of the Prophet's greatness and bravery and austere living." He was introduced to Theosophy as well and grappled with Madame Blavatsky's *Key to Philosophy*, and Mrs Annie Besant's *How I became a Theosophist*.

Mohandas passed his examinations and was called to the Bar on 10th June, 1891 and enrolled in the High Court on 11th June. Before his departure from London, he hosted a farewell dinner for friends from the London Vegetarian Society, a vegetarian meal in the Holborn Restaurant on Kingsway. While the dinner went off very well, his plan to set the table roaring with laughter with a humorous sally in his after-dinner speech was foiled by his shyness and stage-fright getting the better of him. He had intended to relate the oft-quoted opening words of Addison's maiden speech in the House of Commons, "I conceive, I conceive, I conceive," but when he was still fumbling for what to say next a wag stood up and said, "The gentleman conceived thrice but brought forth nothing." Poor Mohan could go no further and finally managed to say, "I thank you gentlemen, for having kindly responded to my invitation," and sat down. It was only in South Africa that Gandhi was able to overcome this hesitation in making speeches before audiences. *The Vegetarian* was, however, gracious in its report about the dinner, saying that "Mr Gandhi, in a very graceful but somewhat nervous speech, welcomed all present, spoke of the pleasure it gave him to see the habit of abstinence from flesh progressing in England, related the manner in which his connection with the London Vegetarian Society arose, and in so doing took occasion to speak in a touching way of what he owed to Dr Oldfield."

The young barrister sailed for Bombay aboard S.S. *Oceania* on 12th June. As he recognized, he "had read the laws, but not learnt how to practise law." The crucial test lay ahead.

★ B. R. Nanda: *Mahatma Gandhi – A Biography*, George Allen and Unwin, London, 1958

On arrival in Bombay Mohandas was received by his elder brother, Laxmidas, who broke the tragic news of the death of their mother Putlibai. She had passed away while he was still in England, but this information had been deliberately withheld from Mohan to spare him the cruel shock while he was in a distant land. Mohan had adored and worshipped his mother and her loss was a terrible blow. She had been to him a vision of loveliness, a model of piety and self-sacrifice and the infinite power of her love had been the most outstanding single influence in Gandhi's life. The news was a severe shock. Years later he wrote:

> My grief was even greater than over my father's death. Most of my cherished hopes were shattered. But I remembered that I did not give myself up to any wild expression of grief. I could even check the tears. . . .

Mohan rejoined his family in Rajkot. He discovered that circumstances had changed since his parents' death and the family no longer enjoyed the prestige it had held earlier, during his father's lifetime. Their dreams of Mohandas stepping into his father's shoes as *Diwan* did not seem to be anywhere near realization but Laxmidas had built high hopes on the young barrister on whose education in London the family had spent a fortune. He was confident that everything would be fine after Mohandas's return and that he would build up, he said, a "swinging practice," which would bring the family its former wealth. Rajkot, however, had more than a fair share of lawyers and the prospects did not appear to be very bright in this small town.

The *Modh Bania* caste community had still not excused Mohandas for having cross-ed the sea and undertaken a foreign voyage. The community believed he had been sullied and in expiation of his sins insisted he undergo "ceremonial purification" before being re-admitted to the brotherhood. Mohan did not have much faith in their eccentric beliefs and superstitions but, he agreed to take a bath at Nasik, a holy place on the sacred River Godavari and thereafter, he gave a dinner for members of the community in Rajkot to atone for his "sins". He was then re-admitted to the *Modh Bania* caste community.

Full of the new ideas he had imbibed from the West, Mohan wished to introduce reforms at home. These extended to European dress, footwear, crockery and cutlery and, among other things, oatmeal porridge and cocoa. But when he insisted that his wife Kasturbai, a simple and homely girl, learn to read and write and adopt western social graces, she was up in arms against his attempts to impose his writ and authority.

Writing about this phase of his life later, Gandhi observed:

> My relations with my wife were still not as desired. Even my stay in England had not cured me of jealousy. I continued my squeamishness and suspiciousness in respect of every little thing, and hence all my cherished desires remained unfulfilled. . . . Once I went the length of sending her away to her father's house, and consented to receive her back only after I had made her thoroughly miserable. I saw later that all this was pure folly on my part.

The new-fangled craze for westernization, after superficial training in England, had led to an escalation in the household expenses. Laxmidas was now a mere law clerk with a modest income and as Mohandas had still not started earning, the family was in real financial difficulties, so Mohandas applied for an appointment as a teacher of English in a local high school but was turned down, to his surprise and discomfiture, on the ground that he was not a graduate. Mohan had felt that the fact of his having passed the London Matriculation examination and having qualified as a barrister would balance the scales in his favour.

After this rebuff, Mohandas decided to go to Bombay to study Indian law, to gain experience of the High Court and secure whatever briefs he could in Bombay and to represent any clients that Laxmidas may be able to find for him from Rajkot or Porbandar. Bombay, however, was no easier, as here he was putting himself up, untried and inexperienced, against the city's large number of well-established legal figures and his first case, in the Small Causes Court, ended in disaster. Of this inauspicious debut he wrote:

> I appeared for the defendant and had to cross-examine the plaintiff's witnesses. I stood up, but my heart sank into my boots. My head was reeling and I felt the whole court was doing likewise. I could think of no questions to ask. The judge must have laughed and the other lawyers, no doubt, enjoyed the spectacle. I sat down and told the agent that I could not conduct the case, that he had better engage Patel and have the fee back from me.

This was a shattering experience and he decided not to take up any more cases until he had the courage and confidence to conduct them. His mind was made up and he returned to Rajkot, to the family home.

Mohandas had learnt his lesson. He "found the barrister's profession a bad job – much show and little knowledge". He never entered a court again until he arrived in Africa. But he also made another discovery: he was good at drafting applications and memorials:

> Disappointed, I left Bombay and went to Rajkot, where I set up my own office. Here I got along moderately well. Drafting applications and memorials brought me on an average, Rs. 300 a month."

Rajkot was also the scene of an unpleasant encounter, a result of racial arrogance and discrimination that was to foreshadow his experiences in South Africa. These played a very large part in turning the meek, shy, introverted young man of mediocre attainments into the arch-revolutionary of his age. Laxmidas had fallen foul of the British Political Agent of Porbandar, Mr Ollivant, because of some alleged irregularities during his term of office as secretary and adviser to the state's young prince. Mohandas, it appears, had met Mr Ollivant while he was on a holiday in London, and the conversation had been cordial and pleasant. Laxmidas had prevailed upon Mohan to meet Mr Ollivant and put in a good word for him and Gandhi had agreed to do so for the sake of his brother, even though it went against the grain to ask for favours from what he termed "a trifling acquaintance". In any event, the sahib did not appreciate the idea of a casual acquaintance whom he had met briefly during a visit to London, taking advantage of this and importuning him for favours. Mr Ollivant was impatient and visibly annoyed. When Mohandas insisted on being permitted to state his case, the sahib was livid with rage and asked his peon to throw him out, which he forcefully did. Gandhi went home crestfallen.

Sir Pherozeshah Mehta, a leading legal luminary in the area, happened to be in Rajkot at the time, and his advice was sought to ascertain if any action could be taken against the Agent for his misconduct and display of racial arrogance. He replied:

> Tell Gandhi, such things are the common experience of many *vakils* and barristers. He is still fresh from England and hot-blooded. He does not know British officers. If he would earn something and have an easy time here, let him tear up the note and pocket the insult. He will gain nothing by proceeding against the sahib, and will very likely ruin himself. Tell him, he has yet to know life.

Writing about this incident later, Gandhi stated:

> The advice was as bitter to me as poison, but I had to swallow it. I pocketed the insult but also profited by it. Never again shall I try to exploit friendship in this way, said I to myself. The shock changed the course of my life. I was no doubt at fault in going to that officer. But his impatience and overbearing anger were out of all proportion to my mistake. It did not warrant expulsion.

The "shock" was followed by a change of direction and location as well. Fate, or whatever you may choose to call it, was inexorably drawing him to another continent, where he was to receive many more shocks, and change not only the course of his own life, but the course of history and international relations over a period of fifty years.

Chapter 3
The South African Connection:
—◦❥ The Formative Years ❦◦—

MOHANDAS WAS BECOMING increasingly exasperated with the working conditions in Rajkot and discontented with the general tenor of life in this town in the back-waters of Kathiawar. He had not succeeded to the position of prime minister of Porbandar for which he had been groomed and despite his training as a barrister in London he had not progressed in overcoming his shyness and stage-fright, as he had found to his cost when his attempt to establish himself as a barrister in Bombay had ended in dismal failure. The hopes and dreams of his family, who had staked everything on financing his education in London, remained unfulfilled, and Gandhi was looking for fresh opportunities and for a change.

When an offer of work in South Africa as a legal assistant for one year for £105, all found and free return passage, came in from the blue, he jumped at this God-sent opportunity without hesitation, welcoming the chance to leave India and try his luck in another part of the world. A Muslim merchant from Porbandar, Dada Abdulla Sheth, who had built up a huge business empire in South Africa had requested Laxmidas to send over his London-trained barrister brother to assist his British attorney in dealing with a claim for £40,000 in a court somewhere in South Africa.

Mohan left his wife and sons in the care of his elder brother in Rajkot and boarded a ship for Durban in May 1893.

South Africa, in 1893, consisted of two southern provinces, Natal and Cape Colony under British jurisdiction and in the north, two independent Boer Republics, the Orange Free State and the Transvaal. The Union of South Africa came into being only after the annexation of these Republics by Britain during the Boer War.

Mohan reached Port Natal in Durban towards the end of May. As he descended the gangway he had an air of quiet confidence about him. He was curious about this new country, this new continent, but little could he realize how important a part South Africa was going to play in his life. He could not have imagined at that moment that he would spend twenty years of the formative period of his life here and in the process, he would not only transform the South African scene, but would himself be transformed in a dramatic and unpredictable manner.

Abdulla Sheth, the merchant, was at the quayside to welcome him. He had never met Mohandas and was a little amused when he saw the young Indian lawyer was

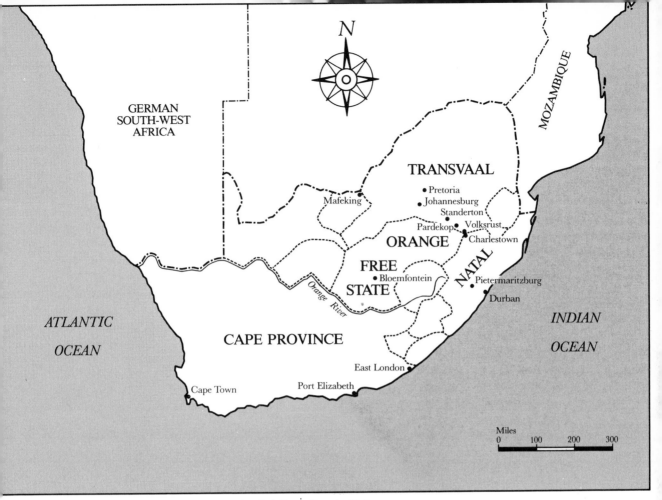

8 South Africa before the Union

wearing a frock-coat, a starched shirt with stiff collar, a black tie and smart shoes. On top of this formal dress, he was wearing a turban. Abdulla must have wondered a little at this apparition, but nevertheless, he received the young barrister very cordially. The legal case in which Gandhi's assistance had been sought was in Pretoria, quite some distance to the North, in the Transvaal, but there appeared no real urgency about proceeding with the case and he invited Mohan to stay on in Durban to meet the members of the Indian community in the city and to familiarize himself with their life-styles, before heading for Pretoria.

It did not take Mohandas long to discover that Indians were not held in much regard in Durban and were treated with scant respect. Racial discrimination was rife and was practised deliberately. During these first days in the city, Abdulla took the young Gandhi one day to see for himself how the administration of justice was carried out in the local law courts. Gandhi was wearing his turban as he took a seat in the courtroom. The magistrate stared at Mohan for a while and then ordered him to remove his turban. As there were other people in the court with turbans, Gandhi re-

9 The newly-qualified barrister in South Africa

garded this as an insult, refused to carry out the order and left the court. The next day he wrote a letter to the editor of a local newspaper lamenting the attitude of the magistrate. This spirited protest was appreciated by many members of the Indian community but evoked considerable caustic comment by hot-heads of the European community, who dubbed him an unwelcome visitor.

After a week in Durban, Gandhi left for Pretoria, travelling by train on which a first class seat had been booked by Abdulla Sheth. The train reached Pieter-maritzburg, the capital of Natal, at about 9 p.m. A European passenger came in, looked at Gandhi and, discovering that he was a coloured man, walked out with a gesture of disapproval, returning a few minutes later with some railroad officials. They ordered Gandhi to remove himself to the van compartment. The officials paid no heed to Gandhi's assertion that he had a first class ticket and on his refusal to get out voluntarily, sought police assistance. The constable came, pushed Gandhi out and the train steamed away, leaving the London-trained Indian "coolie" barrister, stranded, all alone, a very unhappy and bewildered man. To stay on in South Africa or to return to his homeland was the big question that tormented him. As in London his "inner voice" spoke, and his mood and his thoughts that night, which became a turning-point in his life are best explained by Gandhi in his own words:

> It was winter, and winter in the higher regions of South Africa is severely cold. Maritzburg being at a high altitude, the cold was extremely bitter. My overcoat was in my luggage, but I did not dare to ask for it lest I should be insulted again, so I sat and shivered. There was no light in the room. . . .
>
> I began to think of my duty. Should I fight for my rights or go back to India, or should I go on to Pretoria without minding the insults, and return to India after finishing the case? It would be cowardice to run back to India without fulfilling my obligation. The hardship to which I was subjected was superficial – only a symptom of the deep disease of colour prejudice. I should try, if possible, to root out the disease and suffer hardships in the process.

On the morning following the grim resolve in the waiting-room at Maritzburg, he had already started to act. Gandhi sent a long telegram of protest to the general manager of the railway and also informed Abdulla Sheth, who met the general manager immediately and directed the Indian merchants in Maritzburg to see Gandhi. "The merchants," Gandhi wrote, "tried to comfort me by narrating their own hardships and explaining that what had happened to me was nothing unusual. They also said that Indians travelling first or second class had to expect trouble from railway officials and white passengers."

Gandhi resumed his journey to Pretoria and the train reached the next stage, Charlestown, the following morning. In those days, the journey from Charlestown to Johannesburg had to be undertaken by stagecoach. Although Gandhi had a ticket for the coach, his troubles were not yet over. Passengers usually sat inside the coach, but the coach leader, a white man, refused to give a mere "coolie" a seat along with other white passengers. The leader decided to sit inside and offered his own seat next to the coachman to Gandhi, who ignored the insult and agreed to sit there. At about 3 p.m. that day, when the coach had reached another stage, Pardekop, the leader wished to sit where Gandhi was seated. He took a piece of dirty sack-cloth, spread it on the foot-board and motioned Gandhi to his new seat. Gandhi was stunned.

> The insult was more than I could bear. In fear and trembling I said to him, "It was you who seated me here, though I should have been accommodated inside. I put up with the insult. Now that you want to sit outside and smoke, you would have me sit at your feet. I will not do so, but I am prepared to sit inside."
>
> As I was struggling through these sentences, the man came down upon me and began heavily to box my ears. He seized me by the arm and tried to drag me down. I clung to the brass rails of the coachbox and was determined to keep my hold even at the risk of breaking my wristbones. The passengers were witnessing the scene – the man swearing at me, dragging and belabouring me, and I remained still. He was strong and I was weak. Some of the passengers were moved to pity and exclaimed: "Man, let him alone, don't beat him. He is right. If he can't stay there, let him come and sit with us."

The leader scornfully refused, let go of Gandhi's arm but kept on glowering at him and threatening him. Gandhi remembered:

My heart was beating fast within my breast, and I was wondering whether I should ever reach my destination alive. . . . I sat speechless and prayed to God to help me.

Help did come at Standerton, the night halt en route and Gandhi heaved a sigh of relief when Indian merchants turned up and put him up for the night.

Finally, after some further unpleasant encounters, Gandhi arrived in Pretoria but it was during these five exciting days that Gandhi had had his "awakening"; the nervous Indian barrister had turned into a champion for the rights of the downtrodden and subjugated minorities. After calling on the attorney in Abdulla Sheth's case, whom he was supposed to assist, he went into action immediately. He called on Tyab Sheth, a local businessman and with his help convened a meeting of the Indian community of Pretoria to discuss their problems and the need for the formation of an organization to deal with their grievances.

The first meeting was attended principally by Muslim merchants, because there were very few Hindus in Pretoria. The Gandhi who could not plead his client's case in the Small Causes Court in Bombay because of stage-fright and nervousness, had suddenly found that he could make a public speech. This first public speech of his life had as its theme the observance of truthfulness in business. He laid stress on forging unity among themselves and the necessity of forgetting all distinctions between Hindus, Muslims and Christians, Parsis, Gujaratis, Madrasis, Punjabis and Sindhis. He also suggested the formation of an association of all Indian settlers "to make representations to authorities concerned in respect of the hardships of Indian settlers." Gandhi offered "to place at its disposal as much of my time and service as was possible." He was satisfied with the result of the meeting and observed "I saw that I made a considerable impresson on the meeting."

The Association continued to meet regularly and did useful work while in the meantime, Gandhi made the acquaintance of the British Agent in Pretoria and communicated with the railway authorities about the redressing of disabilities under which Indians had to travel. On this point he received a letter from the authorities conceding that first and second class tickets would be issued to Indians who were properly dressed.

Gandhi made a deep study of the social, political and economic conditions of the Indian community in the Transvaal and the Orange Free State, and this useful background was to stand him in good stead, the connections built at this time to prove useful to him in his later public life. The "briefless" barrister of Bombay had turned into a public figure, concerned about the condition of Indians in South Africa, and he describes how these affected him:

I thus made an intimate study of the hard conditions of the Indian settlers, not only by reading and hearing about it, but by personal experience. I saw that South Africa was no country for a self-respecting Indian, and my mind became more and more occupied with the question as to how this state of things could be improved.

It was in Pretoria that Gandhi acquired the "true knowledge of legal practice" and gained confidence in his ability to work as a lawyer, and it was a considerable relief to him to discover that he would not be a failure as a legal practitioner. Gandhi made a careful study of Dada Abdulla Sheth's case and found that both parties, who were closely related to each other, were ruining themselves in litigation and entreated them to accept arbitration. After the arbitrator had given a decision in favour of Abdulla Sheth, he persuaded the successful plaintiff to show lenience to the other party (the same Tyeb Sheth who had helped him organize the local Indian community) by not insisting on an outright payment of the huge sum of £37,000 plus costs but to accept payment by instalments. He was a friend of both the parties and his successful role as a mediator was highly appreciated by them. Gandhi was delighted.

> Both were happy over the result and both rose in the public estimation. My joy was boundless. I had learnt to find out the better side of human nature and to enter men's hearts. I realized that the true function of a lawyer was to unite parties riven asunder. The lesson was so indelibly burnt into me that a large part of my time during the twenty years of my practice as a lawyer was occupied in bringing about private compromises of hundreds of cases. I lost nothing thereby, not even my money, certainly not my soul.

Besides his public and legal activities in Pretoria, the religious spirit within him urged him towards the study of different faiths in an attempt to find the true meaning of religion. Mr Baker, the attorney and a lay preacher, introduced him to many Christian friends and a Mr Coates, a Quaker friend who became very close to him, gave him several books and commentaries on Christian beliefs in the hope of converting Gandhi to the Christian faith. Gandhi relished the study of different aspects of Christianity and engaged in long discussions, but never felt the need to change his religion, in spite of his conviction that Hinduism had as many defects as any other great religion. Of his religious ferment at that time, he wrote:

> It was impossible for me to regard Christianity as a perfect religion or the greatest of all religions. Thus, if I could not accept Christianity either as a perfect or the greatest religion, neither was I then convinced of Hinduism being such. Hindu defects were pressingly visible to me. If untouchability could be a part of Hinduism, it could but be a rotten part or an excrescence. I could not understand the *raison d'être* of a multitude of sects and castes.
>
> As Christian friends were endeavouring to convert me, even so were Muslim friends. . . . I purchased Sale's translation of the Koran and began reading it. I also obtained other books on Islam. I communicated with Christian friends in England. Tolstoy's *The Kingdom of God is Within You* overwhelmed me.

During this time Raychandbhai, his spiritual preceptor in India, was in continual correspondence with him and sent him books to read. Gandhi maintained his friendship with Christian thinkers and said: "Though I took a path my Christian friends had not intended for me, I have remained forever indebted to them for the religious quest they had awakened in me." During the years that followed, the religious quest became more earnest, more pronounced and was to influence his political philosophy.

The lawsuit was over and Gandhi was preparing to return to India, at the end of his one-year contract, when, during the farewell party in Durban hosted by Abdulla Sheth, he was handed a copy of the *Natal Mercury*. It carried a headline about a Bill which would be coming before Natal's new Assembly, a Bill which would disen-franchise Natal's Indians. He turned to the guests who either could not understand or did not care about the implications and said to Abdulla Sheth, "This Bill, if it passes into law, will make our lot extremely difficult. It is the first nail in our coffin. It strikes at the very root of self-respect." The guests responded by persuading Gandhibhai (bhai means brother) to extend his stay and to help the community in fighting off this retrograde legislation. Someone asked about fees.

The mention of fees pained Gandhi and he replied: "Abdulla Sheth, fees are out of the question. There can be no fees for public work. I can stay, if at all, as a servant." Offers of money and volunteers poured in and the farewell party was turned into a working committee. Hindus, Parsis, Muslims responded and felt united as they had never felt before. A campaign was organized and a petition was sent to the Natal Leg-islative Assembly, but despite protests the Bill was passed. Gandhi was persuaded to stay on, and in July 1894 he sent a new petition to Lord Ripon, the Colonial Secre-tary in London, which contained 10,000 signatures. He also wrote to the eminent In-dian Dadabhai Naoroji, who had become M.P. for Finsbury. *The Times* in London, *Times of India* and other papers in India extended support and finally Gandhi's cease-less efforts were blessed with success: Lord Ripon refused assent to the Bill on the grounds that no part of the British Empire could impose a colour bar on another part of the Empire.

It was in 1894 that Gandhi also helped in the setting up of the Natal Indian Congress and became its secretary. Its aim was to promote better understanding between Indian and European citizens in Natal, to introduce Indians to their own history and culture and to engage in social, political and charitable work amongst the members of the Indian community. Later, when Queen Victoria died in 1901, Gandhi sent a message of condolence on behalf of the Indian community of Durban. He also laid a wreath on their behalf on her statue in the city. Another feature was the dissemination of in-formation about the state of affairs in Natal, to the English in South Africa and England and the people of India and the press. With this object in view, Gandhi wrote two pamphlets which dealt with "the real state of things" in Natal and a brief history of the issue of franchise in Natal for the Indian community. Bearing the titles "An Appeal to Every Briton in South Africa" and "The Indian Franchise – An Appeal", these pamphlets were widely circulated.

As Gandhi was held up in Natal on account of public work, he had put in an applica-tion for admission as an advocate of the Supreme Court. It met considerable opposi-tion from European lawyers and the Law Society, who opposed it on technical grounds. The Chief Justice, however, decided in Gandhi's favour and Gandhi set up in practice in Natal.

Gandhi was now a practising lawyer in South Africa, earning in the region of £5,000 to £6,000 a year and in 1896 he decided to go back to India to arrange for his family to join him in South Africa. During his stay he took the opportunity to meet Indian national leaders and acquaint them with the situation in South Africa, and to seek their support for the cause. The Nationalist movement was beginning to grow and was dominated in the 1890s by two leaders, Gopal Krishna Gokhale, a moderate, and Bal Ganga Dhar Tilak, the radical leader. Gokhale and Gandhi took to each other instantly. He also met the editor of the *Pioneer* in Allahabad, who agreed to allot some space for the South African Question in his paper, and when Gandhi had published a pamphlet about the situation in South Africa, the *Pioneer* published an editorial on it and Reuters in turn forwarded a highly-coloured despatch to Natal. The report ran:

> September, 14. A pamphlet published in India declares that the Indians in Natal are robbed and assaulted, and treated like beasts and are unable to obtain redress. *Times of India* advocates an enquiry about these allegations.

Gandhi had said nothing of the kind and had been scrupulously fair, but the report, which had been published in South African papers, had caused great indignation among the members of the European community of Natal. When Gandhi and his family reached Durban some time before Christmas that year, they were forbidden entry. It so happened that aboard the ship in which Gandhi and his family had come over, and in another ship which had steamed in at the same time, were 800 Indians, proceeding to South Africa as a fresh batch of indentured labourers. The Europeans were up in arms against the landing of Gandhi and the large contingent of labourers. The ships were put in quarantine and it took some days of explanation to convince the leaders of the white community that Gandhi had been misreported and that the

10   Members of the Natal Indian Congress, outside the offices of M.K. Gandhi, Attorney

11 The Indian Ambulance Corps founded by Gandhi (*middle row, centre*) during
the Boer War

Indian contingent had not been inducted by him. Eventually, after three weeks, his
compatriots were allowed to land and Kasturbai and the boys were taken separately
to the house of Rustomjee, a Parsi friend. When Gandhi, accompanied by a European
friend, walked out of the ship some trouble-makers recognized him and mobbed him.
He was belaboured, his turban was ripped off and he was kicked and pelted with
stones and bricks until the wife of the police superintendent, a Mrs Alexander,
shielded him with her umbrella and took him to safety. The fateful day was 13th
January 1897 and Gandhi had had a fortunate escape.

In 1899, the Boer War broke out. Gandhi was a loyal subject of the British Empire
and in spite of racial discrimination, which he considered a local un-British aberra-
tion, he felt that Indians could not stand aside. He volunteered to raise an Indian ambulance corps, and after initial hesitation the offer was accepted. A large contingent
consisting of over a thousand Indians under the leadership of Gandhi served honoura-

bly; they were tireless and well-disciplined and on occasions marched over twenty miles a day. Gandhi along with 36 others received medals in recognition of their services.

On the battlefront, relations with the British troops were cordial. Writing about it at a later date he mentioned:

Tommy was altogether lovable. He mixed with us freely. He often shared with us his luxuries, if there were any to be had. There was a spirit of brotherhood irrespective of colour or creed.

After the war, there was no evidence of any change in the political climate and he persuaded the Natal Indians to let him go back to India. This request was conceded by them rather reluctantly on the condition that he would return, in case he was required, within a year. During the farewell party he and Kasturbai were presented with costly gifts, and in spite of his wife's reluctance to part with the gold jewellery she had been given, he decided that all these presents should be sold and utilized by the Natal Indian Congress; a classic example of the high standards of public morality and selflessness that he had set for himself and his family.

Gandhi was back in India on 19th December 1901 and was able to attend the seventeenth session of the Indian National Congress at Calcutta, at which he managed to get a resolution through in support of the struggle for equal rights and removal of

12   (a) Gandhi's Boer War Medal

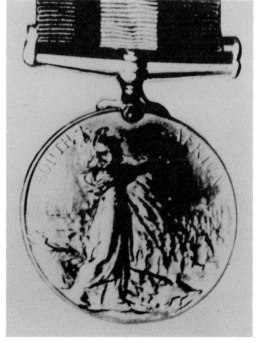

disabilities of the 100,000 British Indians in South Africa.

Before settling down once again, he paid a short visit to Burma and a number of cities and religious centres in India, and after practising at Rajkot for a few months, he moved to Bombay. His life was stable and his practice expanding when, in response to a cable received in 1902 from South Africa, he returned once more.

After meeting Joseph Chamberlain the British Colonial Secretary in Durban, he went on to Johannesburg: he had decided to stay on in the Transvaal and conduct his campaign against racial discrimination from this base. Gandhi was enrolled as an attorney of the Transvaal Supreme Court and it was not long before he was able to establish his practice once again, and with this foundation set about being of service to the members of the Indian community.

In 1903, Gandhi decided to launch a weekly journal, *Indian Opinion*, for dissemination of information in English, Gujarati, Hindi and Tamil. Readers' letters were a valuable source for gauging public opinion and ascertaining which matters were causing most concern. Gandhi strove to educate his readers and in the process educated himself. Henry Polak, a young Jewish lawyer drawn to Gandhi's inner circle of friends assisted Gandhi in his legal work and became a member of the household. Gandhi had to subsidise the paper out of his savings to the tune of £75 per month, a large sum in those days and the Hindi and Tamil editions were dropped as an economy measure. A Lincolnshire man, Albert West, who worked in a small printing concern had also become an adherent to the cause of the Indian community and Gandhi persuaded West to work for *Indian Opinion*. He too became a member of the expanding Gandhi "clan".

During one of Gandhi's long journeys to Durban, Henry Polak gave him Ruskin's *Unto This Last* as reading material. The book overwhelmed him and he decided to bring about transformation in his life in accordance with the teachings of the book. He later on translated the book into Gujarati. Writing about the impact it made on his life he said:

> I believe that I discovered some of my deepest convictions reflected in this great book of Ruskin, and that is why it so captured me and made me transform my life.

Gandhi grasped the central teachings of Ruskin to be: that the good of the individual is contained in the good of all; that a lawyer's work has the same value as the barber's inasmuch as everyone has the same right to earn their livelihood from their work; that a life of labour, that is the life of the tiller of the soil and the craftsman, is worth living.

Gandhi was inspired to put the ideas of Ruskin into action and purchased a hundred acres of land at Phoenix, some fourteen miles from Durban, for £1,000. It was to be run as a kind of agrarian commune. *Indian Opinion* was shifted there and some half a dozen European and Indian families lived on the Phoenix Farm. "It was a miniature republic under Gandhi's spell, whether he was there or not," remarked Geoffrey Ashe in his study of Gandhi★.

★ Geoffrey Ashe: *Gandhi: A Study in Revolution*, William Heinemann Ltd, London, 1968

12   (b) Medal received for his work as leader of the stretcher-bearer corps
during the Zulu Rebellion

During the Zulu wars in the years that followed, Gandhi sold his Johannesburg house, moved his family to the Phoenix Farm, and went once again to war. He raised a party of 25 stretcher bearers, was given the rank of sergeant-major and along with his corps he nursed Zulu victims while regular soldiers made fun of the Indians fussing over the "niggers".

Gandhi had been giving deep thought during this time to the questions of sex and abstinence. He felt that public work required single-minded devotion and in order to acquire this he must attain *Brahmcharya* or total self-control, based upon sexual continence and complete abstention. He decided to take a vow of celibacy so that he could devote all his attention to service of his community. On return from the Zulu war he announced his vow to Kasturbai who acquiesced in silence to this austere vow.

In 1906 the Transvaal Government instituted an ordinance which required Indians to carry registration certificates and residence permits at all times. Gandhi urged the Indian community to resist this obnoxious law and not to register.

The reaction to this threatened oppression was an early example of what was to be Gandhi's single most powerful weapon: satyagraha. Literally "truth force", satyagraha can be inadequately translated as passive resistance or non-violent non-cooperation, and was to be used again and again, first by Gandhi and then by those he influenced, to combat injustice and persecution.

The Indian community was incensed by the attempt to treat them as second class citizens living on suffrance in the Transvaal. Gandhi observed in *Indian Opinion:*

> We are responsible for the safety, not only of ten or fifteen thousand Indians in Transvaal, but of the entire Indian community in South Africa. The fate of the Indians in Natal and the Cape depends on our resistance . . . India's honour is in our keeping. For the Ordinance seeks to humiliate not only ourselves but also India, our motherland.

A mass protest meeting was called and on 11th September 1906 Indians closed their shops. They were ready for the hardship and the penalties that disobedience of the law might entail.

In spite of Indian protests and campaigns, the ordinance was passed, although it had not yet received the Royal Assent. Gandhi, accompanied by an educated Muslim representative, went to London for talks with Lord Elgin, the Colonial Secretary, and Lord Morley, the Secretary of State for India. The King had been withholding assent to the Bill but was likely to be swayed by the fact that South Africa would be getting Home Rule the following March and would then in any way be able to operate without constraint.

The Permit Offices in Johannesburg opened on 1st July 1907. The approaches were picketed and with the exception of a very small number, the Indians refused to register. Gandhi was sentenced to three months' hard labour, plus a fine or further imprisonment. While he was in prison, Gandhi was taken to Pretoria for talks with General Smuts, who promised to repeal the act as soon as the majority of the Indian community had undergone registration. Gandhi went back to his supporters and appealed to them to register, a decision which amounted to a volte face and not appreciated by many of his followers, and when Gandhi went, on 10th February, to the head of the queue for registration, he was brutally mauled by a Pathan, Mir Alam. Reverend Doke, an English missionary who was an admirer of Gandhi, took him to his own house and nursed him and when the Registrar of Asiatics arrived at Mr Doke's house Gandhi became the first to register. Within a few days all Indians had registered.

The General had, however, not honoured his pledge, by repealing the Act. Gandhi was shocked by this treachery and issued an ultimatum that if the repeal was not carried out by 16th August, the registration certificates would be consigned to a bonfire. Accordingly, at 4 p.m. on the appointed day, the Indians in the city of Johannesburg assembled in front of the Haminia mosque and the certificates were consumed in the fire in the cauldron. The *Daily Mail* in London hailed it as another Boston Tea Party.

Things had come to a stand-still. Gandhi and another member of the deputation, Haji Habib, left for Britain to seek intervention. In 1912 Gokhale, who had become a member of the Viceroy's Executive Council in India, arrived in South Africa on an official visit to ascertain the state of affairs for himself. He was also assured that the Black Act would be repealed, but still nothing happened. Instead as if to add fuel to the fire, a judicial decision was announced that in future only Christian marriages registered in South Africa would be considered as valid, thus invalidating all Hindu, Sikh, Parsi and Muslim marriages and making all off-spring of these marriages illegitimate. It was this final insult that decided Gandhi to go into battle by launching a satyagraha campaign. Hermann Kallenbach, a German architect and Gandhi's

13   Gandhi with his secretary, Miss Schlesin, and his German friend, Herr
Kallenbach. South Africa, 1913

Stopped at Border Volksrust.

14   Crossing the state line at Volksrust, in defiance of the law

friend and admirer, acquired a 1,100-acre farm near Johannesburg and placed it at the
disposal of Gandhi for use by satyagrahis. It was christened the Tolstoy Farm. By
1913 Gandhi decided to launch his final campaign in which parties of volunteers from
Natal and the Transvaal were asked to cross into each other's state without permit
and thereby court imprisonment. The Indian miners in Newcastle went on strike and
their employers started using all kinds of nefarious tactics to break them up but they
had unflinching faith in Gandhi and nothing could stop them from playing their part.
Gandhi was arrested, bailed out, rejoined the strikers and was re-arrested, bailed out
again as the cycle repeated itself. He was subjected to all kinds of indignities and severe
hardships to break his spirit but he held firm.

Lord Hardinge, the Viceroy of India, lodged a protest about the maltreatment of
Indians in South Africa and asked for the institution of a Court of Enquiry.

The arrival at this time of Charles Freer Andrews and Willie Pearson from Santiniketan in India was of great help to Gandhi. Gokhale had issued an appeal in India
for volunteers for help in South Africa and these two great friends and well-wishers
of India, who were teaching and participating in the cultural life at the Centre and
the University founded by the poet Rabindranath Tagore, had volunteered to come
to South Africa and help Gandhi in his campaign. Charlie Andrews, who had gone
to India as an Anglican priest to lecture at St Stephen's College, had terminated his
connection with the Church of England and stayed on in India to serve the country.

Willie Pearson, a congregational minister at Cambridge had also gone to India as a missionary, but had resigned. Like C. F. Andrews he came under Tagore's spell and stayed on in Santiniketan. Charlie Andrews became a very close and life-long friend of Gandhi. He was of great help in mediating between Gandhi and Smuts and the achievement of agreement was finally greatly facilitated by the efforts of Andrews. The major points which had given rise to the launch of the satyagraha campaign were conceded: the £3 poll tax was removed, marriages performed according to Indian customs and traditions were recognized as valid, and registration formalities were simplified and standardized. The satyagraha campaign was called off.

General Smuts wrote in 1939 that it had been his "fate to be the antagonist of a man for whom even then I had the highest respect." As for the satyagraha movement, he recalled: "Gandhi himself received – what no doubt he desired – a short period of rest and quiet in gaol. For him everything went according to plan. For me – the defender of law and order – the odium of carrying out a law, and finally, the discomfiture when the law had to be repealed."

15 C.F. Andrews (*left*) and W. Pearson were staunch supporters of Gandhi in South Africa and in India

Chapter 4
India Observed:
—◆▸ Experiments in Satyagraha ◂◆—

THE GANDHI WHO finally bade goodbye to South Africa, on 18th July 1914 was quite a contrast with the shy young Mohandas who had landed in Durban in 1893. The South African odyssey had transformed him into a highly respected statesman of lofty moral stature. Gandhi was overwhelmed by the tributes paid to him by his compatriots and Europeans during farewell gatherings and banquets all over the Union Territories and on the actual day of his departure a farewell ceremony for Kasturbai and himself, presided over by the Mayor of Durban, was held in the Town Hall. He said that he would retain very pleasant memories of his days in South Africa, but General Smuts was obviously relieved at Gandhi's departure; in a letter to a friend he mentioned: "The saint has left our shores, I hope for ever." Gandhi never visited South Africa again, but was to make a poignant reference in 1924 to "the painful contrast between the happy ending of the satyagraha struggle and the present condition of the Indians in South Africa", in his book *History of Satyagraha in South Africa*.

Gokhale had asked Gandhi to meet him in London before returning home to India and Mohandas, Kasturbai and their German friend, Kallenbach, therefore sailed for England that summer. They learnt in Madeira that war was likely to break out any moment, and Gandhi and his party arrived in London on 6th August, two days after the declaration of war. Gokhale had been stranded in Paris and Kallenbach, who was still a German citizen after 18 years in South Africa, was sent, despite Gandhi's frantic appeals to the India Office on his behalf, to an internment camp and was therefore not able to accompany Gandhi to India as planned. A reception was held at the Hotel Cecil on 8th August by Gandhi's friends and admirers in honour of "the hero of the South African struggle". Amongst those who attended and paid tribute to Gandhi were Mohamed Ali Jinnah, then a rising political star, who subsequently became the founding father of Pakistan, and Mrs Sarojini Naidu, the poet, who became a life-long admirer and devotee of Gandhi. Mrs Naidu, whose poems had been published in two volumes, *The Golden Threshold* and *The Bird of Time* was an extrovert, with

16   Mrs Sarojini Naidu

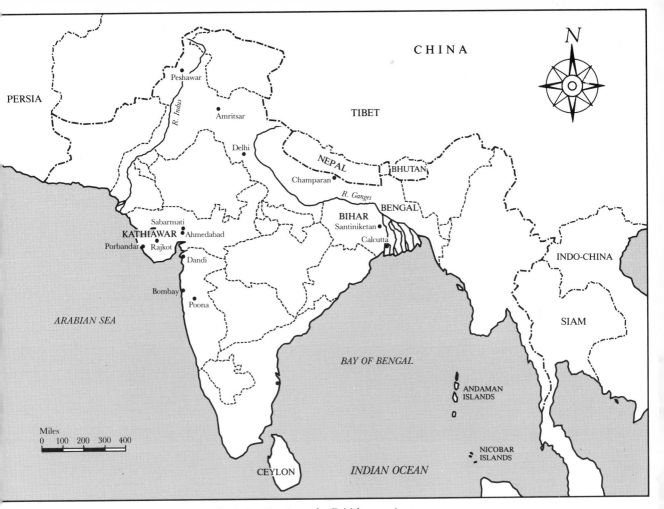

17   The Indian Empire under British sovereignty

a delightful sense of humour of whom Robert Payne, the American biographer of Gandhi, said: "[she] would be remembered as a political figure who was devoted to Gandhi and strong enough to stand up to him when he was being wildly erratic. She like to call him 'Mickey Mouse'. When he was in danger or when he was fasting, she would defend him like a tigress defending her young. Exuberant, earthy, irreverent, improbable, she was one of those women who make the world glad."★

Gandhi had the same regard for British sense of justice and fair play, that he had displayed in South Africa. It was against his moral principles to take advantage of, or embarrass, Britain while she was involved in a war or a crisis, even though he detested her colonial stranglehold on India.

> I thought that England's need should not be turned into our opportunity, and that it was more becoming and far-sighted not to press our demands while the war lasted . . . I felt that Indians residing in Britain ought to do their bit in the war.

Gandhi's appeal for help to his compatriots met with success, and he wrote to the

★ Robert Payne: *The Life and Death of Mahatma Gandhi.*

Under Secretary of State offering their services towards the war effort. This was appreciated and the offer of help at that critical hour was accepted. It was decided to raise a Field Ambulance Corps and about eighty Indian volunteers started a period of six-week training courses in first aid. Gandhi was the unofficial chairman of the Volunteer Corps and had intended to stay on in England to be of service, but a serious attack of pleurisy prevented him from doing so. He listened to the advice of friends and decided to return to India. He was distressed to find that Kallenbach could not accompany him and Gandhi later stated that "it was a great wrench parting from Mr Kallenbach, but I could see that his pang was greater."

On 9th January 1915, Mohandas Karamchand Gandhi returned home with Kasturbai by S.S. *Arabia* and he was given a spectacular hero's welcome. Huge crowds had gathered at the Apollo Bunder in Bombay and he was met on board by a deputation of the city's élite, and hundreds waited on the quayside to shout their vociferous greetings. When he landed he was wearing *swadeshi* (of one's own country) dress consisting of a Kathiawari cloak, a turban and dhoti.

A magnificent reception attended by over 600 distinguished citizens of Bombay, representing almost every community in the city, was held in honour of the Gandhis in the palatial surroundings of Jehangir Petit's house. Gandhi felt, he said, "absolutely out of element" amidst the elegance and sophistication of the westernized élite of Bombay, and the pomp and splendour of Petit's house. Sir Pherozeshah Mehta, Bombay's leading barrister, paid tribute to the qualities of head and heart, the sacrifices and achievements of Gandhi and of Kasturbai, the "heroine of South Africa", who had stood shoulder to shoulder with her husband throughout the struggle. In his reply, Gandhi stated with absolute frankness that he had felt more at home among the indentured labour in South Africa than among the aristocratic and sophisticated citizens of Bombay. At many subsequent receptions reference was made to Kasturbai as "the wife of the great Gandhi" which Gandhi had countered by saying that he had no knowledge of "the great Gandhi." There was a special reception held by the Gujarati community and Jinnah delivered an admirable speech in English on the occasion. Most of the other speeches were also in English. When it came to Gandhi's turn to thank the audience he did so in Gujarati rather than in English, declaring that he preferred to speak Gujarati and Hindi among Gujarati audiences.

In a press interview he announced: "I propose to remain in India and serve the motherland for the rest of my days." About his immediate plans, he stated that he had been away for a long time and would spend a year as an observer, in accordance with the advice given to him by his political guru, Gopal Krishna Gokhale.

Before leaving for Poona to see Gokhale, he called on Lord Willingdon, the Governor of Bombay on a courtesy visit: the Government of India had also joined in honouring Gandhi by awarding him a Kaiser-i-Hind gold medal in the New Year Honours List of 1915.

Gandhi had first met Tilak and Gokhale, the two leading lights of the nationalist movement in India, in 1896. He had developed an instant admiration for Gokhale and recording his impressions of this meeting, said

He [Gokhale] gave me an affectionate welcome, and his manner immediately won my heart. With him . . . this was my first meeting, and yet it seemed as though we were renewing an old friendship. Sir Pherozeshah [Mehta] had seemed to me like the Himalaya, Lokmanya like the ocean. But Gokhale was as the Ganges. One could have a refreshing bath in the holy river. The Himalaya was unscalable, and one could not easily launch forth on the sea, but the Ganges invited one to its bosom.

Gokhale had indeed taken Gandhi to his bosom; he became his friend, philosopher and guide and was of invaluable help to him during the South African struggle. Gokhale was highly impressed by Gandhi's work in South Africa and had prophesied: "One day you will, I hope, see a man who is destined to do very great things for India", and on his return home, it was to his political mentor that Gandhi turned for advice before entering the Indian political scene. In 1905 Gokhale had founded the Servants of India Society and by 1915 it consisted of a small band of carefully selected social workers dedicated to selfless service to the motherland. Gokhale wanted Gandhi to join the society, and he was himself quite keen to do so, but several members of the society voiced doubts that Gandhi's belief in extra-constitutional methods, his loudly-voiced apprehensions about the benefits of modern science and technology and in fact his whole approach, would fit in with their aims and objectives. While Gandhi was received by Gokhale and the members of the society very warmly, the question of his membership was kept pending. When Gandhi mentioned to Gokhale his desire to found an ashram, so that he could settle down with his fellow-countrymen from the Phoenix Farm who had returned to India before him and were staying temporarily at Santiniketan, Gokhale made an offer to meet all expenses. This came as a great relief to Gandhi, who had been worried about the problem of financing the project.

From Poona, Gandhi proceeded to Rajkot to visit friends and relations, and a month later he was on his way to Santiniketan in West Bengal to meet Rabindranath Tagore, the great poet and celebrated Nobel Prize winner. Tagore had established a school devoted to the cultivation of music and fine arts, and an international university which attracted scholars and students from many countries. Set in idyllic surroundings about forty miles north of Calcutta, in an ashram-like atmosphere, Santiniketan, which means "the abode of peace", was a flourishing community when Gandhi arrived. The poet was away but Gandhi was warmly received by the community, meeting once again his old friend, Charlie Andrews who was teaching there and who had arranged for the twenty members of the Phoenix Ashram to settle under Tagore's kind and gracious eye.

Gandhi had hardly been a week at Santiniketan, when the tragic news of Gokhale's sudden death was received. He and Kasturbai left immediately for Poona. Gandhi had lost a "sure pilot" in Gokhale, on whom he had been depending for guidance through the coming upheavals in Indian political life.

The question of his membership of the Servants of India Society was still unsettled and so Gandhi, deciding against pursuing the matter further, returned, after brief visits to Calcutta and Rangoon, to Santiniketan and Tagore.

18   Rabindranath Tagore, the Bengali poet and Nobel Prize winner

19   Gandhi visits Tagore at Santiniketan

The poet, who was known as *Gurudev* (reverent teacher), was majestic in flowing robes, bearded, tall and handsome, passionately devoted to music, poetry and the fine arts, and imbued with a great love for his country and humanity at large. Tagore the literary giant and one of the leading pioneers in the renaissance of Bengali literature and arts, was an admirer of Gandhi and the two men, so different from one another in approach, found they shared many common aims, as Geoffrey Ashe observes:

> In some respects the two were alike. The poet's faith in the peasantry, his longing for a village rebirth put him closer to Gandhi than to most of the Indian politicians. They had certain loathings in common – child-marriage, for instance. Nor was the visitor a philistine. He had kept his love of music and poetry. Yet when he moved in on the gracious flower-bedecked school, its whole character altered. As a wise American woman once remarked, "Tagore was like the mountain and Gandhi like the cataract going down to the people below".★

It was Tagore who conferred on him the status of Mahatma. Mahatma means a "great soul" and Tagore's lyrical ecstasy in his description of the attributes of the Mahatma is a poet's testimony:

★ Geoffrey Ashe: *Gandhi: A Study in Revolution.*

He stopped at the thresholds of the huts of the thousands of dispossessed, dressed like one of their own. He spoke to them in their own language. Here was living truth at last, and not only quotations from books. For this reason, the Mahatma, the name given to him by the people of India, is his real name. Who else has felt like him that Indians are his own flesh and blood? When love came to the door of India, that door was opened wide. At Gandhi's call, India blossomed forth to new greatness, just as once, in earlier times Buddha proclaimed the truth of fellow feeling and compassion among all living creatures.

Gandhi kept his word to Gokhale and avoided making any comment on political issues during the year of his return, travelled widely all over India and confined his comments to religious and social issues. His most important task was to start an ashram, where he could settle the party of eighteen boys who had come over from the Phoenix settlement in Natal. They were staying at Santiniketan, under the leadership of Magan Lal, a cousin and very able and dedicated lieutenant of Gandhi. The ashram would also accommodate other co-workers who wanted to lead a simple life and serve the community. While suggestions were made for settling down in Calcutta, Hardwar and Rajkot, Gandhi decided in favour of Ahmedabad, because he thought he could render greater service to the country through the Gujarati language. Ahmedabad offered other advantages: as an ancient centre of handloom weaving, it was likely to be a suitable place for revival of the cottage industry of hand-spinning, and there were financial considerations as well, since it was felt that its affluent commercial quarters might be able to help the ashram. The Satyagraha Ashram was founded on 25th May 1915, in the bungalow of an Ahmedabad barrister, Jivanlal Desai, at Kochrab, a village near the city. There were about twenty-five men and women and, apart from those who had come from South Africa, were some who had come in from different parts of the country. All had their meals in a common

20   Sevagram: Gandhi's room at the ashram

kitchen and strove to live as one family. A code of rules and observances was drawn up for the ashramites and they were expected to observe the vows of truth, *ahimsa*, celibacy, simple living, non-possession and selfless service.

The number of ashramites increased and the bungalow was soon neither suitable nor adequate for the community. With an occurrence of plague in the village, the ashram was moved to a permanent site on the banks of the Sabarmati river where the new ashram covered an area of 150 acres. Cottages for all the essential requirements, which included a school, a dairy farm and craft centre, besides provision for spinning and weaving, were achieved with the generous financial assistance of industrial houses in Ahmedabad and Bombay.

But the stability of the ashram was soon to be threatened by Gandhi's own magnanimity. A family of untouchables – Dudabhai, a teacher in Bombay, his wife Danibehn and their daughter, wished to join the Satyagraha Ashram and had been referred to Gandhi by Amritlal Thakkar of the Servants of India Society. Their acceptance into the ashram created uproar. Kasturbai, who had only reluctantly agreed to accept an untouchable's presence in her home in South Africa, herself raised the banner of revolt and Magan Lal, the indefatigable organizer, also joined in the protest. While Gandhi was able to overrule them and restore peace, the business community of Ahmedabad, on whose beneficence the ashram relied, disapproved of Gandhi's reformist zeal and withdrew their financial backing. The ashram funds dried up and the position of the community became desperate. At this stage, help came from an unexpected quarter and the crisis was averted by an anonymous donation of Rs. 13,000, a great deal of money in 1915. The donor, it was later discovered, was a Mr Ambalal Sarabhai, owner of textile mills and a wealthy businessman in Ahmedabad. Although his period of probation of one year that he had promised to Gokhale was over, most of Gandhi's activities in 1916 consisted of attending conferences and making speeches; he had still to make his debut on the Indian political scene.

The first call for help in fighting oppression came from the Champaran district in Bihar, then a prime producer of indigo. Most estate owners in the area were British and the tenants of Champaran were obliged by law to plant three-twentieths of their land with indigo. In accordance with the *tinkathia* system, the indigo crop had then to be passed on to the landlord as part-payment for rent, and this inequitable feudal practice had been subject to many abuses. The plight of the tenants had been brought to Gandhi's attention and Gandhi, to whom Champaran had been but a name on a map, was soon involved in the public agitation for amelioration in the conditions of these unfortunate victims. Raj Kumar Shukla, one of the farmers of Champaran who had met Gandhi at a Congress meeting in Calcutta, prevailed upon him to visit the area to investigate the situation at first hand. On 16th April 1917, Gandhi arrived in the Champaran district and orders were served on him by the Commissioner of the district to leave the area immediately. Gandhi declined to carry out the order and wrote to the magistrate:

> Out of a sense of public responsibility, I feel it to be my duty to say that I am unable to leave the district, but if it pleases the authorities I shall submit to the order by suffering

21   Kathiawari dress: Gandhi at the time of his early satyagraha campaigns
in India

the penalty of disobedience. My desire is purely and simply for a genuine search for know-ledge. And this I shall continue to satisfy so long as I am free.

All eyes were on Gandhi when he appeared in the Champaran District Magistrate's court on 18th April. He submitted:

> As a law-abiding citizen, my first instinct would be, as it was, to obey the order served on me. I could not do so, without doing violence to my sense of duty to those for whom I came. . . . I have disregarded the order served upon me, not for want of respect for lawful authority, but in obedience to the higher law of our being – the voice of conscience.

The magistrate was nonplussed, released Gandhi on bail and referred the matter to higher authorities. No sentence was awarded because the Lieutenant-Governor of the province considered that "a serious mistake of judgement" had been made by the Commissioner of the Division and passed orders for the abandoning of all proceed-ings against Gandhi. The Commissioner was further directed to provide all possible facilities for the conduct of his investigations.

Gandhi had shot into fame and popularity and was hailed as a hero by the peasants. The planters, however, were highly upset by Gandhi's searching and comprehensive cross-examination and investigation of the reports made by the tenants, who were only too willing to furnish all the details of their cases. The Champaran planters en-gineered agitations against Gandhi and false accusations were made against him and his team of co-workers, but the more they were maligned, the more they rose in pub-lic estimation. The Indian Press greeted him as the liberator, the hero of South Africa who had started the passive resistance campaign over there and had gone to jail. The *Amrit Bazaar Patrika*, a leading English daily from Calcutta commented: "God bless Mr Gandhi and his work. How we wish we had only half-a-dozen Gandhis in India to teach our people self-abnegation and selfless patriotism" and Gandhi was to record in his autobiography: "The Champaran struggle was a proof of the fact that disin-terested service of the people in any sphere ultimately helps the country politically."

The Government of India read the danger signals and asked the Governor of Bihar to appoint an Enquiry Commission to investigate the grievances of the agricultural community of Champaran and to recommend a solution to the problems. Gandhi was invited to serve as a member and in due course the Commission accepted his sug-gestions, which were incorporated in its report. The Committee was unanimous in its recommendation for the abolition of the *tinkathia* system and planters were asked to refund 25 per cent of the money extracted illegally from the tenants. Legislative measures were taken to improve their lot, restrictions imposed to avoid the recur-rence of terrorism and exploitation. The non-violent strike or satyagraha which Gan-dhi had organized so successfully was an object-lesson for everybody: the landlords had used violence for defeating the strike and many peasants had received injuries, but they did not repay violence with violence and had learnt the fearlessness and cour-age of a true satyagrahi; these uneducated and helpless peasants had miraculously shed their fear and gained their self-respect. At the same time Gandhi did not ignore social reform and sent volunteers to the villages to run primary schools and to disseminate information for the improvement of sanitary conditions and hygiene in the rural areas. Six primary schools were opened in the Champaran district and the teachers, who were also volunteers, did not receive their wages in cash but in the form of free food and accommodation.

While the constructive work in the villages of Champaran was the focus of Gandhi's attention, he received an urgent summons for help from the textile workers for guidance in their struggle for higher wages and better conditions from the mill-owners in Ahmedabad. Gandhi knew the mill-owners and suggested to the employers and labourers that they both submit the dispute to arbitration. The appeal on behalf of the workers was made by Anusuyabehn, sister of Ambalal Sarabhai, the leader of the mill-owners who was adamant in his refusal of the wage increase suggested by Gandhi. In the circumstances, Gandhi had no alternative but to urge the workers to go on strike, and laid down rules for strict observance: never to resort to violence; never to molest non-strikers or black-legs; to remain firm and not to give in; never to depend on charity or beg for alms but to try to earn bread by honest labour. The workers took a solemn pledge to continue the strike until a satisfactory settlement had been arrived at.

Gandhi held daily meetings of the strikers on the banks of the Sabarmati River and they came in their thousands, but after two weeks there were signs of a weakening in resolve: hunger and the machinations of the mill-owners were having a demoralizing effect. Gandhi was unhappy about this situation and announced that he would fast if they did not continue the strike. The workers were alarmed at this move and while they did not succeed in dissuading Gandhi from adopting this course, their

22   Nehru and Gandhi spinning, an everyday activity in the Gandhi ashrams

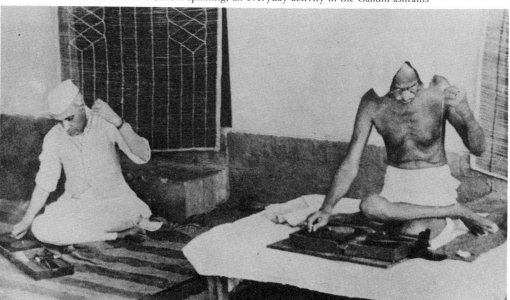

morale received an unexpected boost and the strike continued with renewed vigour. Finally, the mill-owners also were touched by Gandhi's gesture and gave in and agreed to arbitration. The struggle under the leadership of the Mahatma had remained peaceful and non-violent and the satyagraha campaign marked a turning point in the relationship between labour and mill-owners, and continued to exercise a healthy influence in the trade union movement in India.

Hardly had this dispute in Ahmedabad been settled when his help was sought by the peasants in Kheda, where famine conditions because of failure of crops made it impossible for them to pay land revenue. Representations made by peasants to suspend revenue assessment for the year went unheeded. Prominent workers of the Servants of India Society and other leaders, Vallabhbhai Patel, Shankarlal Banker, Anasuyabehn and Mahadev Desai among them, joined Gandhi in the campaign to voice the grievances of the farm workers of this area. Gandhi's suggestion for the appointment of an impartial enquiry committee was turned down and so Gandhi made an on-the-spot study of over fifty villages affected by crop failure and felt that the demands of the peasants were just, and the Government was not doing their duty by them in relieving them of their distress. He advised all farm workers, rich or poor, to refuse to pay revenues and to be prepared for all repressive measures that the Government might take against them, including confiscation of their land and other property. The *patidars* responded to the call. The Government imposed many repressive measures, but the peasants remained firm and unshaken in their resolve. After four months of hard struggle, the Government relented and yielded.

Champaran, Kheda and the Ahmedabad mill-strike had been success stories. The experience gained by the Mahatma in South Africa had been put to good use in India. But another trial awaited Gandhi. World War I was in a crucial phase and the Viceroy invited national leaders to attend a conference in Delhi for extending their support to the war effort. Leaders like Tilak had not been invited. Gandhi hesitated for a while, but finally decided to attend, and made a brief statement in support of a recruitment drive. On his return to Gujarat, he started a vigorous recruitment campaign which involved walking from village to village in the heat and dust of the kutcha village tracks. Many of his associates however, did not share his enthusiasm and the response to Gandhi's appeal was not very encouraging. He would not take proper nourishment and medicine and finally his illness became so serious that he had to interrupt the recruitment drive and return home. It took him quite a while to recover from his illness, by which time the war was coming to a close and the need to go on another recruiting campaign did not arise.

Chapter 5
Gandhi Emerges as
—•❧ National Leader ❧•—

BY THE TIME war ended in November 1918, with victory for the Allies, over one million Indian volunteers had joined forces with the British Army and had played a significant part in the campaigns in the Middle East and Europe. The Government of India had not hesitated in exerting all kinds of pressures and in using coercive measures to collect materials, equipment and finances for the operations, and suppression of civil liberties, internment of political leaders, imposition of heavy taxes, extortion of forced loans, unchecked inflation and heavy prices, and an influenza epidemic which had taken a heavy toll of lives, was the price that the country had paid for the successful culmination of the war in Europe.

Gandhi's action in supporting the war effort, was inconsistent with his own teachings and was questioned by close friends like Charlie Andrews and others, but Gandhi was a great loyalist and his views about the British Empire had never changed. He was a firm believer in its sense of justice and fair play, its democratic values and its generosity towards its subjects. He felt that self-rule would be granted as a "reward for defending the empire." He had written to the Viceroy:

> I recognize that in the hour of its danger we must give, as we have decided to give, ungrudging and unequivocal support to the empire of which we aspire in the near future to be partners in the same sense as the dominions overseas. But it is the simple truth that our response is due to the expectation that our goal will be reached all the more speedily. . . . If I could make my countrymen retrace their steps, I would make them withdraw all the Congress resolutions and not whisper "Home Rule" or "Responsible Government" during the pendency of the war. I would make India offer all her able-bodied sons as a sacrifice to the empire at its most critical moment and I know that India, by this very act, would become the most favoured partner in the empire and racial distinctions would become a thing of the past. . . . I write this, because I love the English nation, and I wish to evoke in every Indian the loyalty of Englishmen.

Gandhi's views about self-rule descending upon India like manna from heaven after the successful conclusion of the war were, however, not shared by Annie Besant, founder of the Home Rule League and herself British by birth, and Tilak, the most radical leader of the nationalist movement. They considered Gandhi's faith in the British Empire naïve and were convinced that Britain would never grant self-rule to India unless she was pushed and had no other alternative.

50

Mahatma Gandhi and other leaders who were hoping for an end to wartime restrictions and a restoration of civil liberties were to receive a rude shock. Instead of making a bold gesture and taking a decisive step towards the direction of granting self-rule to India, as Gandhi had hoped for after the war, the Government of India were on the verge of introducing repressive legislation to crush the movement for Home Rule. During the war a commission headed by Justice Rowlatt had been invited by the Government to make recommendations for combating seditious activities. This was an ill-timed and reactionary step. The Government already enjoyed wide powers under the Criminal Law Amendment Act of 1908, the Press Act of 1910 and the Defence of India Act of 1915 and when the Government published the report containing the recommendations of the Rowlatt Committee in July 1918, it recommended further oppressive measures such as trial without jury or right of appeal, arrest and internment on suspicion and two years' imprisonment for the possession of a seditious document. In the resulting furore throughout the country, the Government ignored the protests as symptoms of "mass hysteria" and hurried the Rowlatt Bill through the central legislature of India, on the strength of its built-in majority of nominated

23 The leader being led: Gandhi with his grandson

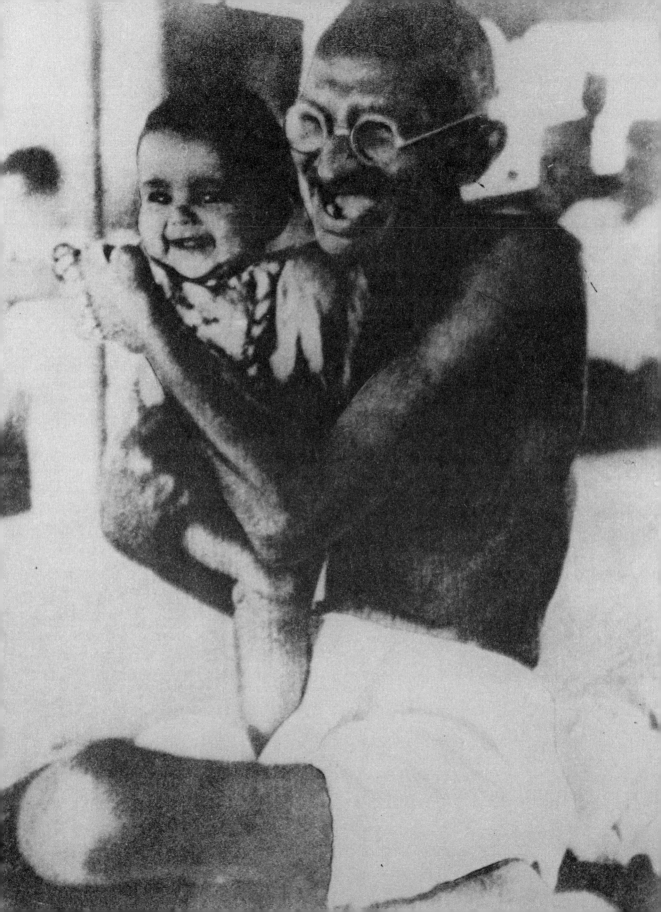

members, and against the united opposition of all elected members. Mahatma Gandhi, who had arisen from his sick-bed and mounted an agitation against the Rowlatt Bill, attended the meeting of the legislature for the first time and noticed the way in which the Bill had been forced through this body. Gandhi met the Viceroy Lord Chelmsford but did not succeed in dissuading him from enacting this oppressive legislation.

Gandhi had kept out of all political agitation on a national scale during the war deliberately, in order not to embarrass the Government in those difficult years. He had made appeals to the public for support to the British during her hour of need and he was disenchanted by this reaction to India's loyalty, as were the moderate Indian leaders who were expecting that India would become a self-governing dominion after the war. Gandhi was a man of action and could not take this onslaught on the dignity and prestige of his fellow countrymen lying down, and in consultation with other political leaders in Madras and Bombay, it was decided to observe a general *hartal* (strike) throughout India. Gandhi relates how the idea was born on the night of 18th March. when he was still in the half-world between sleep and consciousness:

> The idea came to me last night in a dream, that we should call upon the country to observe a general *hartal*. Satyagraha is a process of self-purification, and ours is a sacred fight, and it seems to me to be in the fitness of things that it should be commenced with an act of self-purification. Let all the people of India therefore suspend their business on that day and observe the day as one of fasting and prayer.

He related this to Rajgopalachari (who was later to be Chief Minister of Madras and succeeded Mountbatten as the first Indian Governor-General of India) and he and other friends welcomed the suggestion. The date of the *hartal* was first fixed for 30th March, but was subsequently changed to 6th April 1919.

Gandhi addressed several meetings in the presidencies (provinces) of Madras and Bombay and stressed the non-violent nature of the protest. The *hartal* in Bombay was led by Gandhi himself and the public meeting addressed by him at Chowpatty, attended by several thousands, was a complete success. In addition, as a calculated act of civil disobedience of Government regulations, two of Gandhi's books proscribed in India, were on sale: *Hind Swaraj* and *Sarvodaya*, his Gujarati translation of Ruskin's *Unto the Last*. 40,000 people took part in a huge procession in Chandni Chowk, the main street of Delhi, until troops opened fire when the processionists refused to obey their order to break up. Five Hindus and four Muslims were shot dead.

In Delhi the *hartal* had been observed on 30th March, the date originally selected for the strike. Swami Shradhanand, a much venerated holy man of Delhi who had organized and led the protest march, invited Gandhi to visit Delhi and Gandhi set off on the journey by train, but while he was still en route the authorities in Delhi served an order on him prohibiting his entry into the capital. When Gandhi refused to go back, he was arrested, taken down to a small railroad station, not far from Delhi and returned by another train back to Bombay, where he was set free. News about Gandhi's arrest spead like wild-fire and in some places there was rioting and violence.

24   A moment of relaxation

In Ahmedabad, in particular, there was considerable excitement and the city had been placed under martial law following the reported murder of some Europeans, tearing up of railway lines and burning of public buildings. Gandhi was distressed by the ugly spectre of violence that had erupted but was able to pacify the people of the city and cool them down, when he was allowed by the authorities to address them at a public meeting in the Sabarmati Ashram.

From Ahmedabad, Gandhi went to Nadiad in the Kheda district and, after hearing stories and full accounts of what had happened, he realized that he had unleashed the weapon of civil disobedience on a large scale before the people were disciplined enough and trained for it. He had therefore made a "Himalayan miscalculation", to use his own words, in launching a satyagraha campaign without educating the people about the "meaning and inner significance of satyagraha". Finally, he decided to suspend satyagraha and observed a three-day fast as a penance for his lack of foresight. This was the first time since his return from South Africa that Gandhi had participated in a national protest movement. The satyagraha campaigns in Champaran, Ahmedabad and Kheda had been local and regional issues; Gandhi was now emerging on a national level and the Rowlatt agitations had shown his form as a dedicated campaigner.

In Amritsar, the holy city of the Sikhs in the Punjab, the anti-Rowlatt *hartal* had passed off peacefully. Over half a million Punjabi soldiers had served in the World War and a large number had had an opportunity to see life at first-hand in European countries. They were not very happy about the state of affairs after the conclusion of the war and had not taken the oppression and humiliation easily: already there was seething discontent and the Rowlatt Act had added fuel to the fire. There were peaceful protests, but the authorities felt that an open revolt was in the offing and they were determined to crush it. Early in April, two popular leaders of the Punjab, Dr Kitchlew and Dr Satyapal, went missing after they had been invited to meet the Deputy Commissioner at his bungalow. Rumours were rife about their deportation and a peaceful march was on its way to the bungalow of the Deputy Commissioner, when troops opened fire on the procession, leaving several dead and many injured. Part of the crowd, who were carrying back their dead and wounded, were infuriated by this senseless act, lost self-control and went on a rampage, burning public buildings and offices, murdering five Englishmen and assaulting Miss Sherwood, a school mistress. Sir Michael O'Dwyer, the Governor of the Punjab was convinced that a conspiracy was afoot and sought the assistance of the army in maintaining law and order in Amritsar. Consequently, a Brigadier-General Dyer arrived on the scene with his troops.

On 12th April, General Dyer issued a proclamation in English banning all meetings and processions. Little effort was made to ensure that the proclamation was read or disseminated to the main nerve centres of the citizens of Amritsar. 13th April was Vaisakhi day, an important religious festival, which marks the beginning of the Hindu New Year and a large crowd, estimated to be anywhere between ten and twenty thousand, had gathered in Jallianwala Bagh grounds for the celebrations. This *bagh* in the heart of the city, barely the size of Trafalgar Square in London, had only

25 The walls of Jallianwala Bagh, showing bullet marks from the massacre

one narrow entrance and exit, and it was surrounded by high buildings on all sides. The crowd, who were in a festive, holiday mood were obviously unaware of any ban on meetings and were listening to a speaker standing on the platform. General Dyer, with 90 Gurkha and Baluch troops and two armoured cars, entered the *bagh* and took up positions. Then, without warning, the troops were ordered to fire. The attack lasted ten minutes and 1600 rounds were fired. There was complete panic and because of the very narrow exit, many people could not get away: some 400 people including women and children were massacred and the number of injured exceeded a thousand. It was one of the most brutal massacres in history and the whole of India was stunned.

There was no expression of regret or admission of guilt. On the contrary, martial law was clamped down in the city and a reign of terror began, intending to teach the "natives" a lesson and cripple their political will and capacity for the defiance of authority. All leaders of the public of any consequence were incarcerated. A war of attrition was launched against the people and all opportunities for humiliating them were seized upon and vindictiveness was sometimes taken to ridiculous lengths: in one street in Amritsar, where an Englishwoman had been assaulted, people were made to crawl at the point of a bayonet, and in certain areas, all persons travelling in any kind of vehicle were required to dismount on seeing an Englishman or woman and make their obeisance by bowing low before resuming their journey. Public floggings were a common feature and the punishments were carried out in a sadistic and heartless fashion.

Strict censorship was imposed on the events in Amritsar. Gandhi's request to visit the Punjab was refused. Gradually rumours about the diabolical state of affairs in the Punjab were penetrating the curtain and there was a wave of shock and indigna-

26   Amritsar today: The Golden Temple

tion in the country. Rabindranath Tagore was deeply moved and renounced his knighthood in protest. In a letter to the Viceroy, Lord Chelmsford, he stated:

> The enormity of the measures taken by the Government to quell some local disturbances has with a rude shock revealed to our minds the helplessness of our position as British subjects in India. The disproportionate severity of the punishments inflicted upon the unfortunate people and methods of carrying them out, we are convinced, are without parallel in the history of civilized governments, barring some conspicuous exceptions, recent or remote. Considering that such treatment has been meted out to a population, disarmed and resourceless, by a power which has the most terribly efficient organization for the destruction of human lives, we must strongly assert that it can claim no political expediency, far less moral justification. . . . The time has come when badges of honour make our shame glaring in the context of humiliation, and I for my part wish to stand, shorn of all special distinctions, by the side of those countrymen, who for their so-called insignificance are liable to suffer degradation not fit for human beings.★

The Amritsar massacre had opened Gandhi's eyes and he looked with horror at the British Empire in which he had had so much faith and hope. He stated:

> When a Government takes up arms against its unarmed subjects, then it has forfeited its right to govern. It has admitted that it can not rule in peace and justice . . . nothing less than the removal of the British and complete self-government could satisfy injured India.

He observed a 24-hour fast for the rest of his life on the anniversary of the Amritsar massacre.

The All-India Congress Committee demanded an immediate enquiry into the atrocities in Amritsar and the Government announced the appointment of a commission under the chairmanship of Lord Hunter, a senior judge of the College of Justice of Scotland. General Dyer was found guilty, relieved of his command and sent in dis-

★ Quoted in D. G. Tendulkar: *Mahatma,* Vol. 1, D.G. Tendulkar and Vithalbhai K. Jhaveri, 1951.

grace back to England. Edwin Montagu, Secretary of State for India had observed "Amritsar was a disaster." But the House of Lords thought otherwise and approved of Dyer's conduct – a sword of honour was presented to him by a group of his admirers and he was presented with a purse of £30,000, raised by public subscription, in response to an appeal by the *Morning Post*. The "butcher" of Amritsar had become a hero in Britain and retired with honour, comforted, perhaps, by the happy thought that he had by his deeds helped in the preservation of the British Empire. Had he preserved it or sown the seeds of its destruction and disintegration, the story of India over the next thirty years would reveal. He had certainly succeeded in turning the loyalist Gandhi into the revolutionary national leader of India.

From 1919 onwards Gandhi moved to the centre of the stage in India. The Amritsar massacres became an imperishable historical turning point in the history of India; the tragedy had opened people's eyes and made Gandhi the focus point of the Indian political scene.

The Indian National Congress had not been happy about the way in which the Hunter Commission was expected to function and had boycotted it from the very outset. They had appointed their own enquiry committee which consisted of distinguished lawyers including Motilal Nehru, father of Jawaharlal Nehru. Gandhi, too, was a member and had been invited to draft its report, which he did with meticulous attention to detail and an almost fanatical zeal for honesty and truth in recording evidence, the personal attributes which had already earned him great admiration and respect among his colleagues.

Another development which had pushed him into a key role in national politics was his close friendship and support for the Ali brothers, who were in the forefront of the Khilafat (Caliphate) movement, which was apprehensive about the future of the Caliphate, after the conclusion of the Great War. The Sultan of Turkey, who was the Caliph of the Islamic world, had aligned himself with the Kaiser and with the end of the war and the defeat of Turkey, it was feared that the British would designate Sheikh Hassan, Sheriff of Mecca, as Caliph in place of the Sultan. The Khilafat movement had gathered momentum and the Muslim community in India was highly concerned about the possible dismemberment of the Turkish Empire and its repercussions on the effectiveness of the Caliphate and the Islamic movement in general. The Khilafat leaders sought the support of Gandhi, who gave it most willingly, and asked the Hindu community to co-operate with the Muslims: these were the heady days of Hindu-Muslim unity, which the country had rarely witnessed before but which were not to survive the fight for national independence. Gandhi became very popular with the Muslims and was now wearing two caps, as leader of the Indian nationalists and of the Khilafat movement. Deputations to the Viceroy and the visit of Khilafat leaders to London had not yielded any results. Hindus and Muslims were standing together in their demand for the restoration of the temporal and spiritual powers of the Sultan and the preservation of his status as a protector of the holy places of Islam.

The terms of the peace treaty with Turkey were published in May 1920 and these confirmed the worst fears of the Muslims and their Hindu supporters about the stripping of the Sultan's empire. There was bitter resentment and disillusionment with the British attitude to the question, and they were determined to put heavy pressure on the Government to reverse their decision. After considerable discussions at various levels, the Khilafat leaders fell in line with Gandhi's suggestion for non-violent non-cooperation with the Government. It was to be carried out in four phases: the first phase would consist of surrender and return of all titles, honours medals and decorations awarded by the British; the second phase would consist of stoppage of work by all government officials, withdrawal of children from government-aided schools and suspension of legal work by all legal practitioners; the third step would be to ask soldiers to cease work and the fourth would be stop payment of taxes. Gandhi was a changed man. There was unusual vehemence in his speeches. His faith in the good sense and values of the British Empire as a power of good had been shaken:

> The British Empire today represents Satanism, and they who love God can afford to have no love for for Satan. The Empire has been guilty of such atrocities that, if it did not apologize for them to God and the country, it would certainly perish. I will go further and say that unless it so apologized, it was the duty of every Indian to destroy it.

When Gandhi returned to India in 1915, the nationalist movement had already taken root in India. The Indian National Congress, which ultimately played the major and decisive part in the liberation of India from British rule, had in fact been founded in 1885, by an Englishman, Allen Octavian Hume, with the blessing of Lord Dufferin, then the Viceroy of India. Hume, a retired Indian civil servant felt, along with a number of British liberals who supported the idea, that there was need for an organization which could discuss administrative and economic problems with representative Indians of the upper middle classes. Its first meeting in Bombay was held under the chairmanship of W. C. Bonerjee, a Calcutta barrister. It was a loyal meeting attended by 72 representatives who extolled the virtues of British rule in India. Its second meeting was chaired by Dadabhai Naoroji, who became a member of the British Parliament for Finsbury in 1892. Its moderate leader, Gopal Krishna Gokhale, who had later become Gandhi's political mentor, also was a believer in the beneficial influence of British rule.

By 1900, the Congress had evolved into a representative political organization with local branches and committees. It had, however, remained a talking shop and its pious resolutions demanding constitutional reform had not been very successful. The moderates were being challenged by militants under the leadership of Bal Ganga Dhar Tilak. Annie Besant, the British leader of the Theosophist movement, had identified herself completely with India's aspirations for self-government and had founded the Home Rule League in 1916. Tilak supported the movement and the Besant-Tilak combination dominated the political scene until Tilak's death in August 1920. Gandhi had remained uninvolved in their struggle but by 1920, the Amritsar massacre and the Khilafat movement had changed the situation and Gandhi had already announced at the Muslim Conference in Delhi that he proposed to launch a non-violent civil dis-

27 Annie Besant

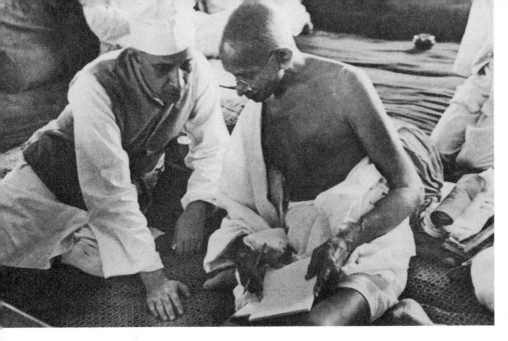

obedience campaign. The special session of the Indian National Congress in Calcutta
in September 1920 adopted the non-cooperation programme advocated by Gandhi,
and the Nagpur session in December 1920 ratified the revised constitution of the Indian National Congress, based largely on Gandhi's own draft. This was a landmark
in the history of the Congress which now became a broad-based organization. The
programme of non-cooperation and constructive work was opposed by many leaders
of the Liberal Party, which included Mr Jinnah, but Gandhi emerged as the unques-
tioned leader of the Congress and remained the people's leader until the achievement
of independence.

   The first stage of the non-cooperation movement was launched with the boycott
of foreign cloth and huge bonfires of imported cloth already in the country were taking place all over India. The Prince of Wales' arrival on a royal state visit in November
1921 was boycotted by the Congress and he was greeted with complete *hartal* and
deserted roads and streets. All the prominent leaders were arrested. 20,000 individual
civil resisters who had offered satyagraha were in jails already. Gandhi was preparing
to launch the mass civil disobedience campaign from Bardoli in Gujarat and had duly
informed the Viceroy about his intentions. Gandhi was now set on a collision course
with the Government when an outbreak of sudden violence at Chauri Chaura, in
Uttar Pradesh, brought the movement to a halt: a clash between satagrahis and the
police resulted in the killing of 22 policemen. Gandhi realized with a shock that the
country was still not yet ready for non-violent struggle and that until his methods
were fully understood there could be further eruptions of violence. He suspended the
civil disobedience movement. Gandhi's jailed colleagues, including Subhash Chandra
Bose, C. R. Das, Motilal Nehru and Lajpat Rai, were bewildered and indignant, distressed at this sudden action because of a stray incident. Jawaharlal Nehru, who was
also stunned by this turn of events and had written to Gandhi from his jail, agreed
after receiving Gandhi's reply and on second thoughts, that in the circumstances Gandhi's decision was right.

Chapter 6
Trial and Imprisonment
—• and the Salt March •—

THE GOVERNMENT OF India, who had stayed their hand when Gandhi was directing
the civil disobedience movement, now decided it was an opportune time to incarcer-
ate him, since he had been discredited on account of the suspension of the movement.
Gandhi was arrested on the evening of 10th March 1922 on the charge of sedition for
three articles written by him and printed in *Young India* with the titles, "Tampering
with Loyalty", "The Puzzle and its Solution" and "Shaking the Manes". Shankarlal
Banker, the publisher of *Young India* was arrested as his accomplice.

The trial was marked by a display of unusual civility and courtesy by C. N.
Broomsfield, the District and Sessions Judge of Ahmedabad, towards the accused,
a polite and dignified statement by Gandhi, ranking among the greatest in the annals
of legal history and a highly courteous response by the judge. Francis Watson's *The
Trial of Mr Gandhi* with a foreword by the late Earl Mountbatten of Burma, contains
a comprehensive background to the case and full account of the proceedings.* The
judge nodded to Gandhi as a sign of respect for him, while he was standing in the
dock and Gandhi made things easy for him by pleading guilty at the very outset and
then, to put in Nanda's words: "In a statement which would have been difficult to
excel in dignified emotion or eloquence, he explained his transition from a staunch
loyalist to a rebel."**

> My public life began in 1893 in South Africa in troubled weather. My first contact with
> British authority in that country was not of a happy character. I discovered that as a man
> and as an Indian I had no rights. . . . But I was not baffled. I thought that his treatment
> of Indians was an excrescence upon a system that was intrinsically and mainly good. . . .
>
> The first shock came in the shape of the Rowlatt Act, a law designed to rob the people
> of real freedom. I felt called upon to lead an intensive agitation against it. Then followed
> the Punjab horrors, beginning with the massacre at Jallianwala Bagh, and culminating in
> crawling orders, public flogging and other indescribable horrors. I discovered too that the
> plighted word of the Prime Minister to the Mussalmans of India regarding the integrity
> of Turkey and the Holy places of Islam was not likely to be fulfilled. . . .
>
> I came reluctantly to the conclusion that the British connection had made India more
> helpless than she ever was before, politically and economically. . . . Little do town-

★ Francis Watson: *The Trial of Mr Gandhi*, Macmillan, London, 1969
★★ B.R. Nanda: *Mahatma Gandhi – A Biography*

29   In the early days, South Africa

30   The Gandhi cap

31   (*below*) Leaving 10 Downing Street, in his "minus-fours

dwellers know how the semi-starved masses of India are slowly sinking to lifelessness. Little do they know that their miserable comfort represents the brokerage they get for the work they do for the foreign exploiter, that the profits and brokerages are sucked from the masses. No sophistry, no jugglery in figures can explain away the evidence that the skeletons in many villages present to the naked eye. . . . The greatest misfortune is that Englishmen and their associates in the administration of the country do not know that they are engaged in the crime I have attempted to describe.

Gandhi pleaded guilty to the charge of promoting disaffection and accepted responsibility for violent outbreaks, and added:

I knew that I was playing with fire. I ran the risk and if I was set free I would still do the same . . . I am, therefore, here to submit not to a light penalty but to the highest penalty. I do not ask for mercy. I do not plead for any extenuating act. I am here, therefore, to invite and cheerfully submit to the highest penalty that can be inflicted upon me for what in law is a deliberate crime, and what appears to me to be the highest duty of a citizen. The only course open to you, the judge, is either to resign your post and thus dissociate yourself from evil, if you feel that the law you are called upon to administer is an evil, and that in reality, I am innocent; or to inflict upon me the severest penalty. . . .

In his judgement the judge observed:

Mr Gandhi, you have made my task easy in one way by pleading guilty to the charge. . . . The law is no respecter of persons. Nevertheless, it will be impossible to ignore the fact that in the eyes of millions of your countrymen, you are a great patriot and a great leader. Even those who differ from you in politics look upon you as a man of high ideals and of noble and of even saintly life. I have to deal with you in one character only. . . . It is my duty to judge you as a man subject to law, who by his own admission has broken the law and committed what to an ordinary man must appear to be grave offence against the law. . . . There are probably few people in India who do not sincerely regret that you should have made it impossible for any government to leave you at liberty. But it is so. . . . You will not consider it unreasonable, I think, that you should be classed with Mr Tilak i.e., a sentence of two years simple imprisonment on each count of the charge; six years in all, which I feel it my duty to pass upon you, and I should like to say in doing so that, if the course of events in India should make it possible for the Government to reduce the period and release you, no one will be better pleased than I.

The finishing touch came from Gandhi. He said:

. . . so far as the sentence itself is concerned I certainly consider that it is as light as any judge would inflict on me, and so far as the whole proceedings are concerned I must say that I could not have expected greater courtesy.

Gandhi did not dislike life in prison, because he could enjoy solitude and enforced rest. It also gave him an opportunity to catch up with his reading, besides keeping up with his morning and evening prayers and spinning – he read constantly, taking in such diverse books as Goethe's *Faust, Man and Superman* by Shaw and Kipling's *Barrack Room Ballads.*

In January 1924, Gandhi had an acute attack of appendicitis and was operated upon by Colonel Maddock, the British Civil Surgeon, at the Sassoon hospital, Poona. The operation was successful and Colonel Maddock and Gandhi became good friends. In response to insistent pressure from the country for Gandhi's release from prison, following his operation, the British Government relented and set him free on 5th February, 1924.

On his release from prison, he was not happy to see Hindus and Muslims drifting apart: Kemal Attaturk had abolished the Caliphate and the Khilafat issue was therefore defunct. Muslims did not need Hindu support any further and there were communal riots in several places, only temporarily appeased by Gandhi's fast for 21 days as a penance for the communal rift. The Congress party itself was a divided house: Das and Motilal Nehru had formed a separate Swaraj party and there was considerable confusion in the political scene.

Gandhi decided to devote himself to constructive work at the Sabarmati Ashram. The ashram population had risen to over a hundred and later touched a peak at over two hundred.

Geoffrey Ashe writes:

Gandhi attracted social workers, scholars, minor politicians, students and cranks. The sole common factor was his [Gandhi's] spell. Many were temporary residents who did not take the vows. There was much tension and argument, and some rivalry for his favour, which he damped down with tact. In admitting applicants, he was not fastidious. He harboured atheists and bigots. He even harboured believers in violence. Some of the ashramites were quite evidently deranged. A visitor asked Gandhi why he wasted time on them. He replied: "Mine is a mad house and I am the maddest of the lot. But those who can not see the good in those people should have their eyes examined."*

It was Gandhi who said, "India lives in her villages and not in her cities." and "When I succeed in ridding the villages of their poverty, I have won Swaraj." He now devoted all his energies to a programme of uplifting Harijans, the implementation

* Geoffrey Ashe: *Gandhi: A Study in Revolution*

32 Gandhi's cottage at the Sevagram ashram became the headquarters for his village reconstruction programme

of a comprehensive plan of village reconstruction and promotion of Hindu-Muslim unity. He had always felt that political, social and economic freedom must be striven for together. He had therefore withdrawn from agitational politics and focused all his energies on the constructive programme.

During these years he made extensive tours of the whole country, making use of all kinds of available transport ranging from the railway trains to bullock-carts, but yielding pride of place to walking, which gave him a unique opportunity to discover the remotest and most inaccessible corners of India. He was venerated by the millions as a saint or an *avatara* (God's incarnation) and this attempt at deification and blind adoration caused him considerable unhappiness and embarrassment. The Mahatma-ship thrust upon him, which he never really accepted, was a severe ordeal and he disclaimed possession of any supernatural or divine powers, beyond the moral and spiritual excellence that all human beings are capable of achieving with dedicated effort. He was a social reformer and urged the people to get rid of the cankers of communalism, untouchability and many other evils that had crept into Hinduism. His repeated advocacy of the extensive adoption of the spinning-wheel and his insistence on the use of *khadi* (hand-spun and hand-woven cloth), was an integral part of his ideas for economic regeneration in rural India. The spinning-wheel and *khadi* were not fads, but symbols which would mark the beginnings of a great revival of cottage industries in India, which had declined as a result of unbridled competition from the products of the industrialized countries. Eighty per cent of India's population lived in its villages. There was not enough land to go around and a very large proportion of them were landless; even those who had land were underemployed for six months of the year. This huge labour force could, he reasoned, be usefully employed on rural crafts and rid themselves of their dependence on the moneylender and diminish their despicable poverty.

In 1920, he turned his attention to the writing of his autobiography, *The Story of my Experiments with Truth*, in Gujarati. It was translated into English by his brilliant and dedicated disciple and secretary, Mahadev Desai, with the help of Pyare Lal, who took over as Gandhi's secretary after Mahadev's death. They were assisted in this task by Srinivasa Sastri, who had succeeded Gokhale as the head of the Servants of India Society and was a life-long friend, philosopher and guide, and also by Madeleine Slade, daughter of a British Admiral who had taken Gandhi as her guru and mentor and whom Gandhi had adopted as his daughter.

The chapters of the autobiography were published week by week in *Young India* to which Gandhi contributed regularly. This book covers Gandhi's life until 1920, as Gandhi felt that there was no need for a sequel because, he said, "thenceforward my life has been too public." It was not Gandhi's wish to write an account in the sense or the genre that autobiography is generally known to western readers. He was concerned primarily with his experiments with "truth" in life. Gandhi wrote about the book and the experiments:

> I claim for them nothing more than does a scientist, who though he conducts his experiments with the utmost accuracy, forethought and minuteness, never claims any finality

about his conclusions. . . . I have gone through deep self-introspection, searched myself through and through . . . yet I am far from claiming any finality about my conclusions.

It is the story of an ordinary boy who grows by sheer will-power and determination and by the force of his circumstances into a leader of supreme stature, adored and venerated by millions of people in his country and throughout the world.

John Haynes, the distinguished American Unitarian leader, published the book in serial form in his weekly *Unity* and Charlie Andrews later also published a version of the autobiography, edited by him, in 1930-31. Henry Polak, H. N. Brailsford and Lord Pethick-Lawrence focused their attention on the book in their volume on Mahatma Gandhi: "It ranks among the world's great books written in prison. In the frankness of its self-revelation, it recalls Rousseau's *Confessions*. . . . In this book Gandhi will live for posterity as the noblest and bravest character of our time." *

In the meanwhile, things were moving once again, with the appointment of the Simon Commission, a Royal Commission, in 1927 by the Conservative government, then in power in Britain. Its object was to review the progress made in constitutional reforms towards self-government in India, in consequence of a clause contained in the Morley-Minto Indian Reforms Act of 1919, which laid down that the position should be reviewed in ten years' time. Apart from Sir John Simon, the Commission consisted of back-bench members, the most prominent of whom was Clement Attlee, the future Labour Prime Minister. It was an "all-white" commission and no Indian had been invited to participate in its deliberations. This was deeply resented by Indians and the Indian National Congress decided to give it the cold shoulder and boycott it. Other political parties in the country also protested against the visit of the Commission to India and the Central Legislative Assembly joined in the boycott by passing a resolution by 68 votes to 62. Its most vigorous opponent was Lajpat Rai, the great leader, a brilliant and powerful speaker, who was called the "lion of the Punjab". He had been the President of the annual session of the Indian National Congress in 1920, which had accepted non-violent non-cooperation as its policy and brought Mahatma Gandhi to the forefront in the national scene. Belonging to the old guard, he was held in great respect. The Government in India paid no heed to the boycott resolution of the Central Legislative Assembly or the protests of political parties and decided to deal with the situation by a show of strength.

When the Commission arrived in India on 3rd February 1928, they were greeted by black-flag demonstrations, slogans of "Simon Go Back", *hartals* and protest meetings. The Government tried to break up the demonstrations by police beatings and Lajpat Rai was assaulted by a young British officer and succumbed to his injuries a few days later. The vicious attack on Lajpat Rai fanned the flames of public indignation, it united the Indian National Congress and the discordant elements returned to the fold, in the wake of injured national feelings. The Simon Commission ended in a fiasco and there was a new wave of public resentment against foreign rule in the country. The boycotting of foreign cloth (from Lancashire) assumed a new frenzy

* H.S. Polak, H.N. Brailsford and Lord Pethick-Lawrence: *Mahatma Gandhi,* Odhams, 1931

33 1928: Angry demonstrations against the Simon Commission

and again public bonfires of foreign cloth all over India reduced imports of cloth from England to about one third of its previous level. This led to the closing down of textile mills in certain areas in the north of England and an increase in unemployment. The change of government in England was followed by the appointment of a new Viceroy, Lord Irwin, who wanted to undo the damage done to relations with India by the insensitive despatch of the Simon Commission. Lord Irwin announced on arrival in India that Britain's ultimate aim was the granting of Dominion Status for India, and that a Round Table Conference would be convened in London to discuss the matter.

The Indian National Congress took umbrage at this patronizing gesture and passed a resolution at its annual session in 1929 declaring *Purna Swarajya* (complete independence or self-rule) to be its ultimate goal of policy. A pledge to this effect was taken all over India at public meetings on 26th January, 1930. For seventeen years this day was celebrated all over India as Independence Day until August 1947. The actual transfer of power to India took place on 15th August that year and henceforth became the Independence Day. However, because of the symbolic association of 26th January, when India chose to become a Sovereign Democratic Republic, this day was chosen for the inauguration of the Republic, and is now known and celebrated as Republic Day. Most of the festivities and celebrations associated with an independence day are centred around 26th January, which is a national holiday and the true day of independence, 15th August, also a national holiday, is marked with comparative restraint.

The country waited for Gandhi's next move and it was dramatic. Manufacture of salt in the country was a state monopoly: no one was permitted to manufacture salt by extraction from sea water. It was the most common element in a poor villager's diet and with the imposition of excise duty and the ban on individual manufacture of sea salt, considerable difficulty was experienced, particularly by those at the bottom end of the social scale. Gandhi decided to try this as a test case for launching a civil disobedience campaign. On 12th March 1930, after having informed the Viceroy, Gandhi embarked on the historic salt march to Dandi, 241 miles away, to manufacture salt in open defiance of Government legislation. It seemed a trivial issue, but the manner of its execution, and its symbolic value in wilful disobedience of government legislation, fired the imagination of the whole nation. The march on foot by

34   On the Salt March to Dandi

78 members of the ashram took 24 days and by the time they reached Dandi, India and the whole world watched the progress of the pilgrims of non-violence. On 6th April, Gandhi and his followers went to the beach after their morning prayers. Gandhi picked up a lump of salt in contravention of the law of the country. This simple act was the signal for defiance of the law by thousands of simple villagers and city-dwellers. They offered themselves for arrest and within a matter of weeks, 100,000 men and women were in jails. Gandhi was also arrested on 4th May. It was a non-violent and peaceful campaign but the Government was shaken by the unexpected strength and vigour of this sudden outburst over the "trivial" issue of salt tax.

A Labour Government was in power once again in Britain. They wanted to hold discussions in London regarding India's progress towards internal self-government. The first session of the Round Table Conference, held in December 1930, was attended by Indians nominated by the Viceroy. In the absence of the Congress leaders in jails in India, its deliberations came to naught. The Prime Minister, Ramsay Macdonald, was hoping that Congress leaders would be represented at the next meeting in London in August 1931. Lord Irwin had a meeting with Mahatma Gandhi and a pact called the Gandhi-Irwin Pact was concluded between them on 5th March 1931. In accordance with this pact, prisoners would be released, the manufacture of salt would be permitted and the civil disobedience campaign would be withdrawn. While no promise was made by the Viceroy regarding the eventual independence of India, it was agreed that the Congress would be represented at the Second Round Table Conference in London. The Pact was the successful culmination of Gandhi's salt campaign and for the first time people living near the sea were allowed to manufacture salt.

Gandhi sailed for England as the sole delegate of the Congress. As he embarked, he warned his colleagues, "There is every chance of my coming back empty-handed." He was accompanied by his secretary, his youngest son, Devdas and Mirabehn (Madeleine Slade). Madeleine Slade, who had been well-known in London social circles during her youth, was one of those unusual women who had given up everything for the spartan life of the Gandhi ashram. She responded to an inner call for a life of dedication to Gandhi and had arrived at the ashram in 1925, at the age of 33. She changed her life-style, adapted herself to the frugal and hard life of the ashram, to Indian food and dress and served Gandhi and India with rare dedication and devotion, for many years. Gandhi had adopted her as his daughter, and she took the name Mirabehn. She has narrated her life story, her absorbing passion for the music of Beethoven, her meeting with Romain Rolland, her spiritual association with Gandhi and India and her eventual return to Austria in her book *The Spirit's Pilgrimage.**

During his stay in London, Gandhi did not stay in a hotel, but was based at Kingsley Hall, in the East End, as the guest of Muriel Lester, the social worker who was in charge of this Social Service Centre for the poor. This provided him with an opportunity of living amongst the ordinary British people for whom he did not change his

* Longman, London, 1960. Mirabehn was recently awarded with the distinguished title of Padma Vibhushan in recognition of her services to the nation.

35   The second Round Table Conference, London, 1931

life-style or dress. He obviously enjoyed his stay and delighted in cutting jokes with the newspaper men who followed him everywhere.

When asked by someone, why he chose to wear a loin cloth only, he replied, "You wear plus fours, mine are minus fours." He wore his "minus fours" when he went to have tea with King George V and Queen Mary in Buckingham Palace and when a reporter who was obviously incensed by Gandhi's cheek in going to Buckingham Palace in his informal dress, asked if he thought he had enough on, Gandhi replied with a smile, "The King was wearing enough for both of us."

Rawding mentions in his book on Gandhi:

> He had talks and meetings with many politicians and people in public life, and thoroughly enjoyed himself. His wit, humour and gentleness, and the purity and sincerity of his character made a great impression on everyone he met. He spoke at several public meetings of his dream of independent India. In Lancashire, the centre of Britain's cotton industry, where his swadeshi policies for cloth-making in India had been one of the causes of great unemployment, he spoke to some of the unemployed. He was received with great affection even here and the mill-workers and their wives came out to cheer him.★

★ F. W. Rawding: *Gandhi,* Cambridge University Press, 1980

36   London, 1931: Gandhi meets Charlie Chaplin

37   Cheers from mill workers in Lancashire

The Conference did not meet with success. There was deadlock over the transfer of defence and foreign affairs, about which the British had reservations and another sticking point was the representation of Muslims and Harijans. On his return journey, he visited Romain Rolland, in Switzerland, who had introduced Gandhi to Europe through his excellent biography. On the day he reached Bombay he said:

I am not conscious of a single experience throughout my three months' stay in England and Europe that made me feel that after all East is East and West is West. On the contrary, I have been convinced more than ever that human nature is much the same, no matter under what clime it flourishes, and that if you approached people with trust and affection you would have ten-fold trust and thousand-fold affection returned to you.

However, the new Viceroy, Lord Willingdon, believed in the adoption of tough policies for crushing indomitable spirits. Nehru, who was travelling to Bombay to

38 Romain Rolland,
Gandhi's first
European biographer

receive Gandhi, was arrested on the way. Gandhi commented: "These are Christmas gifts from Lord Willingdon, our Christian Viceroy." A week late Gandhi was also arrested and detained in Yervada Jail, without trial.

While he was behind prison walls he learnt that the British Government proposed to introduce separate electorates for untouchables. Gandhi wrote to Ramsay Macdonald, the British Prime Minister, that this would be a suicidal course to follow and would not be of help to the Harijans, since it would lead to polarization between Hindus and Harijans. He embarked on a fast until death to undo the damage. The Mahatma's fast was not directed against the British, but against the rigid ostracism practised by caste Hindus. The conscience of the Hindu community was pricked and there were frantic parleys between the leaders of the caste Hindus and Dr Ambedkar, leader of the Harijans, and a pact was signed between the two parties. This formula was also accepted by the British Government and the Mahatma agreed to end his fast. For the next six years Gandhi devoted his energies to the improvement of the condition of Harijans and the implementation of the village reconstruction programme, which had been interrupted by his sojourn to London and his imprisonment.

Chapter 7
Quit India:
—◦⟩ The Parting of the Ways ⟨◦—

WITH THE OUTBREAK of war in Europe in September 1939, the Viceroy of India declared that India was at war with Germany. No Indian representative was consulted in the matter, and even though his declaration was an exercise of his Viceregal powers, it was considered tactless to impose a war on four hundred million people without even an informal consultation with them. Nehru and other prominent leaders were opposed to "fascist expansionism" and had been critical of the "appeasement policy" of Neville Chamberlain. There is no doubt that they would have stood shoulder to shoulder with Britain in the conduct of the war and the defence of democratic values and institutions, but much had happened in India since the unilateral declaration of war in 1914 and the mood of the people in 1939 was quite different. Jawaharlal Nehru wrote in *The Discovery of India*★

> The idea of a great country like India being treated as a chattel and her people utterly and contemptuously ignored was bitterly resented. Was all the struggle and suffering of the past twenty years to count for nothing? . . . One man, [the Viceroy] and he a foreigner, could plunge 400 millions of human beings into war, without the slightest reference to them. There was something fundamentally wrong and rotten in a system under which the fate of these millions could be decided in this way. In the Dominions the decision was taken by popular representatives after full debate and consideration of points of view. Not so in India, and it hurt.

★ J. L. Nehru: *The Discovery of India*, Signet Press, Calcutta, 1946

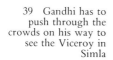

39 Gandhi has to push through the crowds on his way to see the Viceroy in Simla

Lord Linlithgow, the Viceroy, invited Gandhi to meet him for discussions on the first day after the declaration of war, perhaps to make amends for this grave omission in consulting him. Gandhi made it clear that his sympathies lay with Britain and it could count upon his moral support; he shuddered at the thought of the possible destruction of Westminster Abbey and the Parliament buildings by bombs. At the same time he made it clear that although his sympathies were "wholly with the allies", he believed "all war to be wholly wrong", and was convinced that non-violence alone, could "save India and the world from self-extinction." His belief in the efficacy of non-violence was so strong that he had even tried to dissuade Hitler from going to war. He was not expecting a reply and in fact never did receive one. He blamed Hitler for starting this war, and on 24th December 1941 wrote an open letter to him. A brief extract from the letter reproduced by Payne in his book on Gandhi affords us an interesting and significant revelation of Gandhi's views at the time.*

> Dear Friend,
>
> That I address you as a friend is no formality. I own no foes. My business in life for the past thirty-three years has been to enlist the friendship of the whole of humanity, by befriending mankind, irrespective of race, colour or creed.
>
> . . . We have no doubt about your bravery or devotion to your fatherland, nor do we believe that you are the monster described by your opponents. But your writings and pronouncements and those of your friends and admirers leave no room for doubt that many of your acts are monstrous and unbecoming of human dignity especially in the estimation of men like me who believe in universal friendliness. Such are your humiliation of Czechoslovakia, the rape of Poland and the swallowing of Denmark. I am aware that your view of life regards such spoliations as virtuous acts. But we have been taught from childhood to regard them as acts degrading to humanity. Hence we can not possibly wish success to your arms.
>
> But ours is a unique position. We resist the British Imperialism no less than Nazism. If there is a difference, it is in degree. Our resistance to it does not mean harm to the British people. We seek to convert them, not to defeat them on the battle-field. Ours is an unarmed revolt against British rule. But whether we convert them or not, we are determined to make their rule impossible by non-violent non-cooperation. . . .
>
> In non-violent technique, as I have said, there is no such thing as defeat, it is all "do or die", without killing or hurting. It can be used practically without money. . . .

Gandhi was also conscious of many of his compatriots' feelings that while Britain was fighting for the defence of democracy and individual rights, India was being denied these very freedoms. When it was suggested that "Britain's difficulty was India's opportunity", and it was the right time to strike back, Gandhi showed his utter abhorrence for such attitudes: "we do not seek our independence out of Britain's ruin. That is not the way of non-violence." While Gandhi remained a pacifist, his colleagues in the Congress leadership were prepared to participate in the war effort on the basis of equality with Britain. The Working Committee of the Congress in its session in September 1939 declared that while they were in full sympathy with those who were "resisting Nazi aggression" and were prepared to cooperate with them,

---

*   Robert Payne: *Life and Death of Mahatma Gandhi*

India could only do so as a free country, "by mutual consent". It invited the British Government "to declare in unequivocal terms their war aims and their views about democracy and, in particular, how these were to apply to India during the war period and after." Gandhi commended the Working Committee's proposals, even though these represented a departure from his views on non-violence and war, since he did not wish to impose his views on others. While his own belief in non-violence was deeply held, the Indian National Congress had accepted it only as a policy for the attainment of a certain objective; they had not finally renounced war or accepted the proposition that the country could be defended in all eventualities by non-violent methods alone. Since the Congress was not prepared to follow Gandhi's line on the effectiveness of non-violence against armed aggression, and was prepared to cooperate with the Government in the prosecution of war, the Mahatma felt that he could not associate himself any longer with a policy in which he had no faith. He therefore entreated the Congress Working Committee to relieve him of his responsibilities and asked for the complete severance of his official connection with the Congress. The Working Committee recognized that there were radical divergences in approach and ideals and they agreed most reluctantly that:

> While the Working Committee hold that the Congress must continue to adhere strictly to the principle of non-violence in their struggle for independence, the Committee . . . have come to the conclusion that they are unable to go to the full length with Gandhiji but they recognize that he should be free to pursue his great ideal.

Nehru, for whom Gandhi had great affection and in whom he had great hopes as the person who was most eminently suited to lead the nation towards freedom, now emerged as the leader of the Congress. Nevertheless, in spite of Gandhi's formal severance with the Congress, no major decisions were taken without his advice and the Congress leaders, Nehru, Patel and others would turn to him for guidance and inspiration, wherever he happened to be in India at a particular time.

When Gandhi met the Viceroy on behalf of the Congress Working Committee and pleaded with him for the acceptance of their resolution, he replied that England was not in a position yet to "define her war aims" and all he could promise at that moment was "consultation at some future date with the ultimate goal of dominion status." The Working Committee was not satisfied with the answer and decided against participation in the war effort, instructing the Congress ministries in the provinces to resign. The Government did not dissolve the legislatures and order fresh elections but assumed direct control of the administrations through the imposition of the Governor's rule. The Working Committee decided to launch a civil disobedience campaign and approached Gandhi once again to assume leadership. Gandhi agreed to organize the campaign. In March 1940, the Muslim League met at Lahore under the leadership of Jinnah and voted for a separate state as its goal. Jinnah had welcomed the decision of the Congress ministries in the provinces to resign and the supporters of the "two nation" theory celebrated the day as the day of deliverance: Mohamed Ali Jinnah had established himself. In Geoffrey Ashe's words: "The mystique of the

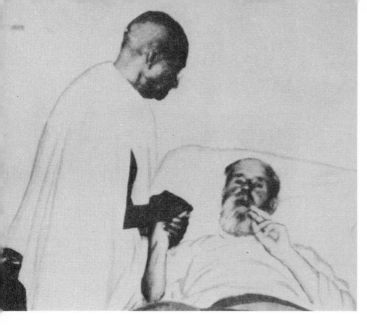

40   C.F. Andrews on his
     death-bed

two nations was enthroned, and Mohamed Ali Jinnah was the Anti-Mahatma. It had taken him nineteen years."★

In April 1940, Gandhi went to Santiniketan to see Charles Freer Andrews, who had been seriously ill for some time. It was to be the last meeting between these two life-long friends and Gandhi's tribute to him on his death was very moving:

> Charlie Andrews was one of the greatest and best Englishmen and because he was a good son of England, he also became a good son of India. When we met in South Africa, we met as brothers and remained as such to the end. It was not a friendship between an Englishman and an Indian. It was an unbreakable bond between two seekers and servants. . . . How can India hate Englishmen as such, when there is the example of Charlie Andrews before us.

In a further consultation with Gandhi in June 1940, Lord Linlithgow offered expansion of the Viceroy's Executive Council and the offer of dominion status at the end of the war, but Congress would not accept the new offer of the Viceroy, as they had demanded an "unequivocal declaration of complete independence at the end of the war and immediate setting up of a Provisional National Government at the Centre". On 17th October, Gandhi launched a civil disobedience movement based on individual disobedience, which would not embarrass the government in the middle of the war. The individual satyagrahis, who were carefully chosen by Gandhi himself, were supposed to make public speeches of protest against the war and offer themselves for arrest. No mass demonstrations were organized. The first person to offer satyagraha was Vinoba Bhave, a learned scholar and faithful disciple who was a believer in non-violence by conviction: Vinoba Bhave was to carry on Gandhi's torch in the field of constructive work and the *Bhoodan* (land-gift) movement, after Gandhi's death. Bhave was followed by Jawaharlal Nehru and other leaders until 2,500 individuals had been arrested. In December 1941, the Government released all the Congress prisoners.

★   Geoffrey Ashe: *Gandhi: A Study in Revolution*

During the early months of 1942, the Japanese forces had been marching triumphantly across South East Asia and had reached Burma soon after the fall of Singapore. A Japanese invasion of India was regarded as a distinct probability. While there was a section of people in the country who were looking upon them as possible liberators, this small minority did not have any love lost for the Japanese, but rather were mesmerised by the romantic story of Subhash Chandra Bose, one-time President of the Indian National Congress and an acknowledged leader of Bengal who, escaping from India, had made his way to Germany and then to Japan. He had organized an Indian National Army from among the ranks of soldiers who had surrendered to the Japanese in Singapore and other volunteers and with this army was poised for a march into India. In spite of this, the majority were opposed to Japanese advance into India and wished to resist any intrusion by their forces.

Winston Churchill as war-time Prime Minister of Great Britain, was implacable in his hostility to the granting of independence to India; he had been agitating against transfer of power to India since the Thirties. B. R. Nanda writes:

> In Britain, Winston Churchill was carrying on a crusade against handing over the people of India to an "oligarchy of lawyers, politicians, fanatics and greedy merchants." "We ought to make it perfectly clear," he said, "that we intend to remain rulers of India for a very long and indefinite period and though we welcome co-operation from loyal Indians, we will have no truck with lawlessness."★

When the "oligarchy" had reared its head again in 1940, he had responded similarly: "I have not become the King's first minister in order to preside over the liquidation of the Empire." Churchill had nothing but contempt for Gandhi's attempted storming of the citadel and had used uncharitable language and powerful rhetoric to denounce Gandhi:

> It is alarming and nauseating to see Mr Gandhi, a seditious Middle Temple lawyer, now posing as a fakir of a type well-known in the East, striding half-naked up the steps of the Viceregal palace, while he is still organizing and conducting a defiant campaign of civil disobedience, to parley on equal terms with the representative of the King-Emperor.

But President Roosevelt had also raised the question of Indian freedom with Churchill, and Chiang Kai Shek, too, made reference to India's struggle for independence, and with the Japanese on India's doorstep. Churchill partly relented. Sir Stafford Cripps, a left-wing socialist who was known to have personal sympathy for India's aspirations to freedom, had been invited to join the war cabinet, and in a fresh gesture to India, Sir Stafford was despatched with a package which came to be known as the Cripps Proposals. Before he left London, he had invited the India Conciliation Group for discussions. Horace Alexander of the Society of Friends in London (Quakers), a close friend of Gandhi since 1928, when he had met him in his ashram in India and author of several books and pamphlets on the Mahatma, was invited to take the chair at the meeting convened to confer on the proposals. In his excellent study, *Gandhi Through Western Eyes,* he writes:

★ B. R. Nanda: *Mahatma Gandhi*

The Cripps proposals were, of course, secret; no hint of their content reached the press until they were presented by him to the Indian leaders. . . . As far as I recall, we did not offer any special comment or suggestions; but Agatha Harrison, our indefatigable secretary, who even in wartime managed to keep a close watch on Indian opinion, with special emphasis on Gandhi, expressed grave doubt about the adequacy of the proposals. A year earlier, they might have been acceptable; but she said once again, they would prove to be late. She was right.★

Gandhi, who met Cripps in Delhi, did not approve of the proposals which, while promising dominion status after the war, would have led to India's balkanization and disintegration as a Union or Federation. The proposal for the setting up of a central administration on an immediate and interim basis was also not satisfactory. Gandhi left for his ashram after a couple of days, while the Congress and other organizations – the Muslim League, the Hindu *Mahasabha* (association) *Ambedkarites* (followers of Ambedkar, the Harijan leader) and others – were deliberating on the plan. It was found to be not acceptable and the Cripps mission ended in failure. The plan had been described as "a post-dated cheque on a bank that was crashing."

The situation was deteriorating. Japanese troops, spearheaded by Subhash Bose's Indian National Army, were advancing towards the Indian border. People were getting restive and Gandhi was apprehensive about an outbreak of violence if the tide was not given direction and kept under control. The British were not ready to entrust India's defence into its own hands. Gandhi asked the British to quit India and was drawing up plans for the organization of a satyagraha campaign. Addressing the session of the All-India Congress Committee that took this historic decision on 7th August, Gandhi had said: "Our quarrel is not with the British people; we fight their imperialism. The proposal for the withdrawal of British power did not come out of anger. It came to enable India to play its due part at the present critical juncture." He was arrested once again, on the morning of 9th August, before he had drawn up precise plans for the satyagraha. Other political leaders were also whisked away to the

★ Horace Alexander: *Gandhi Through Western Eyes,* Asia Publishing House, London, 1969

41   1942. Sir Stafford Cripps: a supporter of independence for India, but his proposals were rejected

jails. With the arrest of leaders who were wedded to peace and non-violence, there were serious breakdowns of law and order, and violence erupted to meet violence exercised by its custodians. While the war with Japan was raging furiously, India itself became a vast armed camp and prison-house.

The wholesale arrests of the national leaders led to resentment and the outbreak of popular revolt throughout the country. It resulted in a complete paralysis of normal life and business, and the authorities set about bringing the situation under control by cruel repression. By 30th November 1942 over 1,000 people had been killed and some 3,200 injured in police firing, according to official sources. Over 100,000 people were in prison. Gandhi and his party were interned in the Aga Khan palace. These were not the carefree days of prison life. He was highly disturbed by the escalating violence in the country and the Government allegation that he was a party to the violent outburst in the country. To add to his sorrows, his efficient, faithful, highly intelligent and capable secretary, Mahadev Desai, who had been with him for the last 20 years, died suddenly. Mahadev had a subtle and brilliant mind, and he was not only a secretary but a confidant as well. Gandhi had lost his right hand and this was a terrible loss.

Gandhi and Kasturbai had been married for over 60 years. In spite of their occasional differences, there was a deep invisible silken bond of undying love between them. While Gandhi was able to relax and rest in the solitude of prison, she could never be at ease. She liked being surrounded by children. She had not been well and was highly upset by Mahadev's death, and hated Aga Khan prison. She had suffered many heart attacks and Gandhi showed considerable signs of stress in his acute anxiety about her state of health. She died in his arms a few months later in February 1944. Her last words were, "I am going now. No one should cry after I have gone. I am at peace." A public funeral was not allowed by the Government and she was cremated in the Palace grounds. That night as Gandhi lay in bed his thoughts were about her; "I can not imagine life without her. She was an indivisible part of me, and her going away has left a vacuum which would never be filled."

Kasturbai's death shattered Gandhi's health and since his condition continued to be serious, he was released in May 1944. It took him quite some time to recover his health, but he turned his head once again to the political scene. He realized that the biggest stumbling block in the way of independence was the demand for a separate Pakistan being insisted upon so vociferously by Mr Jinnah. Gandhi had known Jinnah for several years and he decided to meet him and win him over to the cause of independence for a united India. Gandhi must have underestimated the determination of Jinnah to achieve his Pakistan. He met Jinnah several times at his palatial home in Bombay, but no progress was made. He wondered at the cause of Jinnah's intransigence and as far as he was concerned, he was clear in his mind that it was due to the presence of a third party, in this case the British Government, in their midst. The Muslim League would be more realistic, he was sure, and the differences could be settled more easily, after the British had left India.

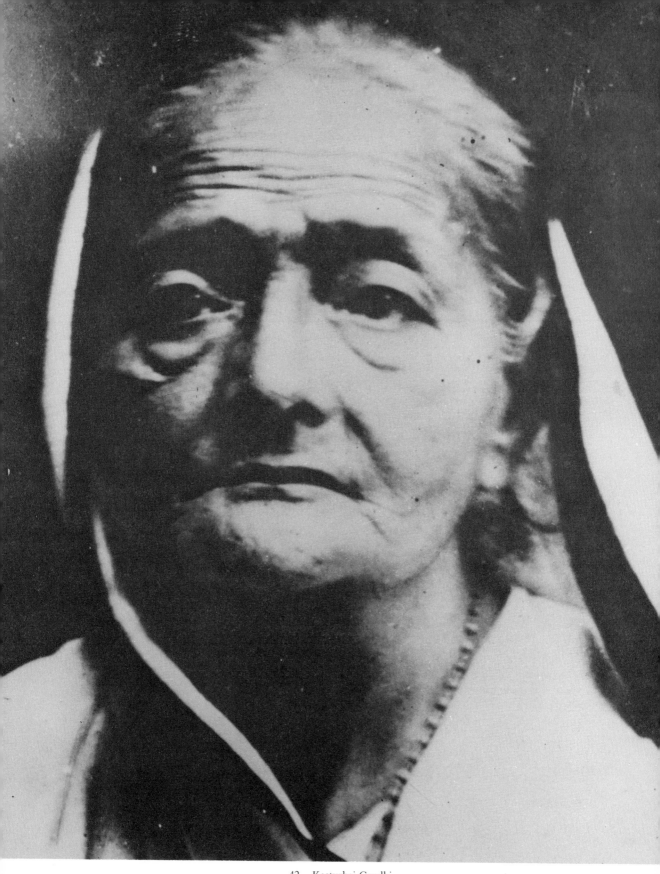

42   Kasturbai Gandhi

Chapter 8
Towards Independence and Martyrdom
—⊶ The World Pays Homage ⊷—

ON THE CONCLUSION of the war in Europe in May 1945, Britain emerged victorious, but exhausted. During the war years, the Indian administration, overburdened by the heavy demands made upon it by the war against Japan and the great strain imposed on it by political tension and unrest, was in danger of losing control. It would have been a formidable task to suppress any further upsurge of political discontent led by the Mahatma or the seizure of initiative by the violent elements. When Mahatma Gandhi was approached by journalists in April 1945 for his views and hopes regarding the United Nations Organization, which was due to meet in San Francisco for its inaugural session to draw up the charter, he spoke quite unequivocally about the significance of the freedom of India:

> Freedom of India will demonstrate to all the exploited races of the earth that their freedom is near and that in no case will they henceforth be exploited.

At the same time he also spelled out his views on war and racial equality:

> There will be no peace for the allies or the world, unless they shed their belief in the efficacy of war and its accompanying terrible deception and fraud, and are determined to hammer out a real peace based on the freedom and equality of all races and nations.

In July 1945, a Labour Government came into power in Britain, under Prime Minister Clement Attlee. This government could not only see the writing on the wall, but was genuinely sympathetic towards India's aspirations for independence. The war had also contributed to the change in the political climate and the British Government lost no time in announcing that it was their intention to grant self-government to India as soon as possible. The Viceroy, Lord Wavell, on his return to India after fresh consultations with the new Government in London, restored provincial rule to popularly elected ministries. The Congress party had secured all the "general" seats throughout the country in the Central Assembly, the Muslim League had won all the specially reserved Muslim seats, made sizeable gains in provinces and captured power in Bengal. Jinnah reiterated his demand for Pakistan, a separate homeland for the Muslims of India. Conceding this demand would lead to the vivisection of India, an ideal completely alien to the Mahatma's belief in Hindu-Muslim unity and brotherhood.

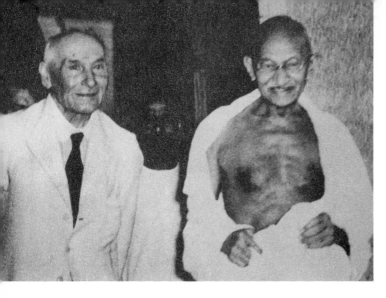

43 Meeting with Lord
Pethick-Lawrence,
1946

A British Cabinet Mission consisting of Lord Pethick-Lawrence, the Secretary of State for India, Sir Stafford Cripps, now President of the Board of Trade, and A. V. Alexander, the First Lord of the Admiralty, arrived in India in March 1946 to prepare the programme for the expeditious transfer of power to India. The Mission held consultations with Mahatma Gandhi and he conveyed his personal view that it would not be easy to achieve agreement between the Hindus and Muslims and other minorities and special interests like the Princes, in the presence of the British ruling power, and suggested that they should hand over power to any party, even Mr Jinnah and quit. Once the British were not on the scene, realism would prevail, he reasoned, and the various elements would adjust and arrive at a mutual agreement in a spirit of give and take. This advice was however not acceptable to the Mission who preferred to settle for a smoother and more clear-cut transfer of power, before withdrawal from India. Since the Congress and the Muslim League, the former holding out for a united India and the later standing for the partition of India, could not come to any agreement, the Cabinet Mission put forward in May 1946 their own proposals for a settlement. Their plan did not encompass the partition of India but provided scope for the satisfaction of Muslim aspirations within the unified federal structure. Gandhi commended the plan to Congress, even though he did not agree with all its provisions, and despite reservations both from Congress and the Muslim League, they gave a qualified acceptance. Wavell invited the Congress and the Muslim League to join in the forming of an interim federal government and since Jinnah refused to join, Nehru became Prime Minister of India in September that year. Jinnah was furious at this turn of events and the Muslim League declared that 15th August 1946 would be observed as Direct Action day, for the achievement of Pakistan, by Muslims all over India. What "Direct Action" meant was not clearly specified, but it was obviously intended that all the weapons in their armoury would be used for the achievement of their objective.

The immediate result of Direct Action was the outbreak of violence in Calcutta on a massive scale which led to an unprecedented massacre of Hindus by Muslims and Muslims by Hindus. The *Statesman* of Calcutta described it as the "great Calcutta

44 Mohamed Ali Jinnah, leader of the Muslim League, in London, December 1946

killing". The toll was heavy – over 5,000 killed and almost 15,000 injured in a matter of a very few days. In Calcutta, the Hindu and Muslim communities were equally matched, but the communal virus now infested the Noakhali district in East Bengal, where Muslims formed the overwhelming majority. Hindu men, women and children were forcibly converted and killed by the thousands. Women were brutally raped and whole villages were set on fire. The stories of these atrocities spread like wild-fire in the neighbouring province of Bihar, where Hindus formed the majority community. There they began to torture Muslims and to ape their Muslim brethren in East Bengal, even to excel them in violence and massacres.

Gandhi was in Delhi at the time of the eruption of this frenzied fratricide and mass hysteria. He was horrified to hear the tragic and blood-curdling accounts of these sinister events. This communal blood-bath was the very negation of his life-time work of promotion of Hindu-Muslim unity, and he could not rest in Delhi while Bengal and Bihar were aflame. Gandhi was 77, but he set off on this heroic mission to the remote villages and hamlets of Noakhali by boat and on foot to cry a halt to this madness; there was deep anguish in his heart. The path was difficult and the task of winning over bitter enemies, of bringing about communal harmony out of the terrible carnage and destruction by love and sympathy was superhuman. But Gandhi fought the challenge of suspicion and distrust and the magic of his appeal to the better side of human nature, the urge to listen to the "inner voice" worked. Thus began the process of healing. He was winning the battle for the hearts of Hindus and Muslims embroiled in the hate campaigns. He wrote: "I have been a born fighter all my life. I must fight even a losing battle. Every day brought new tales of horror; independence was going to be drowned in innocent blood." While Gandhi's presence in Bihar and Bengal had improved the situation in these two provinces, violence was spreading to other areas and India seemed to be heading for a civil war.

On 2nd February 1947, Attlee declared in the House of Commons that the British Government definitely intended to leave India by June 1948. He added that if no agreement was reached by that time between the parties concerned about the devising of an agreed framework for the administration of the country, they would transfer

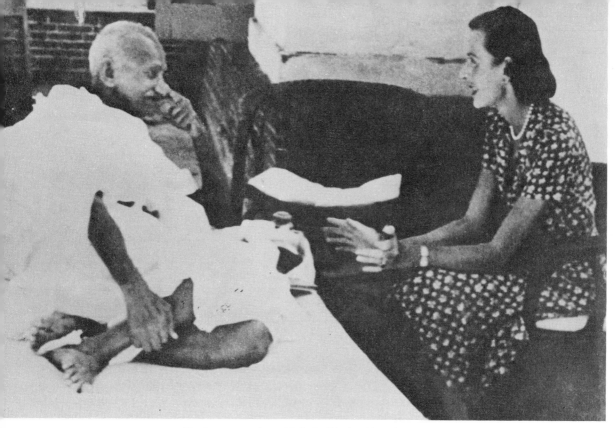

45   In conversation with Lady Edwina Mountbatten

46   Taking tea with Lord Mountbatten

power to some form of central or provincial government as may seem reasonable and in the best interests of the country. Whitehall also announced the appointment of Rear-Admiral Lord Mountbatten, formerly supreme commander in South East Asia, and a close relation of the Royal Family, to succeed Wavell as the new Viceroy. Mountbatten, a "non-party figure" with a reputation for charm and ability was specially selected for carrying out what seemed a very difficult task, and arrived in Delhi with his wife, Lady Edwina, on 22nd March 1947.

Mountbatten invited Mahatma Gandhi to meet him for consultations and while it was quite obvious to him that Gandhi was not willing to agree to the partition of India, he developed an instant admiration for him. Mountbatten described the impact of the first meeting:

> I invited him [Gandhi] to come and see me and he did so just nine days after my arrival. I knew his reputation of course, as an astute and experienced politician. But by then, on the eve of a national fulfilment which for him was marred by the scar of vivisection, he had withdrawn from the front line of political negotiation. I knew also that he was revered by millions as a saint, a Mahatma, a title which, even while rejecting it, he had invested with a new concept or moral responsibility. What I had been quite unprepared to find was a lovable old man, warm, charming, considerate and full of fun.

Jinnah made it quite clear to Mountbatten that he was definitely not interested in the possibility of working for an undivided India, and that a civil war would envelop the whole of India if an independent Pakistan was not set up. Ultimately anarchy and violence and the fear of civil war became the strongest arguments in favour of Pakistan and Nehru, Patel and the majority of leaders of the Congress Party had to readjust their views and accept that they had no choice in the matter and had to accede to the creation of Pakistan, in spite of Gandhi's opposition. Gandhi had no hand in the conduct of the final negotiations. The strength of his feelings is borne out by his statement:

> We are unable to think coherently whilst the British power is still functioning in India. Its function is not to change the map of India. All it has to do is to withdraw and leave India, carrying out the withdrawal, if possible in an orderly manner, maybe even in chaos, before the promised date.

Partition had now been accepted as a *fait accompli* and the date for the independence was brought forward to 15th August 1947. Under the 3rd June plan, power was to be transferred to two successor states, India and Pakistan.

Gandhi was disturbed by the spectre of violence that had been raging off and on in Calcutta since his return to Delhi and feared its recrudescence on 15th August. He was not terribly excited about the independence of the country, for which he had devoted his whole life and felt that there was greater need for him in Calcutta on that date than in the capital, where the independence day would be heralded with pomp and pageantry. The Mahatma's presence in the town electrified the atmosphere and Hindus and Muslims celebrated the eve of independence on the streets of Calcutta. They sang and danced together and displayed a rare spirit of fraternization and

47 15th August 1947.
Independence Day outside
the Red Fort, Delhi

camaraderie. This was in marked contrast to the scenes in West Punjab (Pakistan) and East Punjab (India) where, in probably the biggest migration in history, Muslims from the East moved to West Punjab and Hindus from the West were transferred to East Punjab. Ten million people were on the move amidst unparalleled destruction and massacre. Almost one million people lost their lives. Calcutta and Bengal seemed to be havens of peace and security by contrast. Gandhi had transformed them, it appeared, by the magic and power of love.

A fortnight later, on 31st August, the peace was broken when a violent, angry and abusive mob raided the house where Gandhi was staying and he escaped injury only providentially. Rioting broke out in other parts of the city as well. Gandhi was shaken, not because of any concern for his own personal safety but because of the lapse of the city into violence, after having been such a good example since independence. He decided to use his moral weapon to cleanse the hearts of the people, by going on fast from 1st September until peace was restored to the city. And it worked. Hindus and Muslims were deeply moved by this act of self-sacrifice on the part of the Mahatma; they felt ashamed of themselves and the leaders of all communities gave a solemn pledge for the maintenance of peace and entreated him to break the fast. Calcutta and Bengal regained their poise and remained calm thereafter and the Calcutta fast was hailed as a miracle. Commenting on this fast, *The Times* in London observed: "It did what several divisions of troops could not have done." Over 50,000

48   The swearing-in ceremony, Independence Day

Government House.
~~The Viceroy's House.~~
New Delhi.

26th August, 1947.

My dear Gandhiji,

In the Punjab we have 55 thousand soldiers and large scale rioting on our hands.   In Bengal our forces consist of one man, and there is no rioting.

As a serving officer, as well as an administrator, may I be allowed to pay my tribute to the One Man Boundary Force, not forgetting his Second in Command, Mr Suhrawardy.

You should have heard the enthusiastic applause which greeted the mention of your name in the Constituent Assembly on the 15th of August when all of us were thinking so much of you.

Edwina has gone off today on a courageous mission to the Punjab with Rajkumari Amrit Kaur, to see what they can do to help relieve the suffering and distress among the refugees.

Yours very sincerely,

Mountbatten of Burma

Mr Gandhi.

49   Mountbatten's tribute to his 'one-man boundary force'

troops were engaged in quelling communal riots and disruption in West and East Punjab, yet they could not bring about the peace which Gandhi was able to secure in West Bengal, single-handed. Lord Mountbatten hailed Gandhi as "the one-man Boundary Force in West Bengal."

But by the first week of September, life in Delhi was paralysed by communal riots. This was sparked off by the tales of Hindu refugees from West Pakistan, who had been subjected to violence and maltreatment. The local Hindus vented their spleen on the large number of Muslim residents of Delhi and while the central Government and the police were trying to control the situation, it had got out of hand and assumed menacing proportions. Mahatma Gandhi was back in Delhi and was trying his very best to re-educate, coax and cajole the audience at his prayer meetings to end fratricidal strife. His entreaties and discourses were not producing the desired effect as fast as he would have wished: Muslims would come to him and relate harrowing tales of persecution by the majority community in Delhi. As the metropolitan city of India Gandhi wanted Delhi to provide a good example in fraternity and he decided once again to undergo a fast and thus use moral force to bring the communities together. This fast, which was to be his last, commenced on 13th January 1948. Writing to Mirabehn, he characterized this as his "greatest fast". He said that he was not seeking "the peace of the grave" but a "peace symbolizing the reunion of the hearts." Mahatma's fast brought Delhi and the whole nation to a stand-still. On 18th January, leaders of various communities and parties in Delhi, prominent citizens and politicians, gathered in Mahatma Gandhi's room in Birla House and gave a solemn pledge that full protection would be given to the lives and property of Muslims. Once he was satisfied that the pledge was given in all seriousness and earnestness and would be scrupulously observed Mahatma Gandhi broke his fast with a glass of juice.

While Gandhi was going all out for the protection of the life and honour of Muslims in India, his unpopularity was growing with an extremist section of Hindus who were incensed at the Mahatma's defence of the Muslims and the protective umbrella extended to him. They were not happy, too, about the overwhelming influence Gandhi wielded with the Government and highly resented the payment of £44 million to Pakistan, paid at Gandhi's instance. This amount was due to Pakistan, but it was being held back by the Government on the plea of Pakistan's intransigence in certain directions. This group of people believed in the revival of the glory of ancient Hindu India and considered Mahatma Gandhi, as a friend of the Muslims, an obstacle in the fulfilment of their cherished dreams.

On 20th January, a bomb was thrown at Gandhi during the evening prayer meeting. It exploded at some distance from the Mahatma and he did not pay much attention to it. On the other hand, quite characteristically, he made a plea to the police not to harrass the assailant. When the police got alarmed and tightened the security network, he objected to their searching those who came to attend the prayer meetings. Although Gandhi had said several times that he would like to live to 125, he was not afraid of death. He had told the police officers not to worry about his safety: "If I have to die, I should die at the prayer meeting. You are wrong in believing that you can protect me from harm. God is my protector."

On 30th January 1948, he was late by a few minutes for the evening prayer meeting, because he had been held up a little beyond the schedule by an important meeting with the Deputy Prime Minister, Sardar Patel. He observed strict punctuality and was not obviously happy over keeping the congregation waiting. With his forearms on the shoulders of Abha and Manubehn, he walked to the prayer ground in the garden. About 500 persons had gathered for the evening congregation. He raised his hand and folded the palms together to greet the crowd who returned the greeting likewise. Many rose from their seats and bowed low as a mark of respect. Without warning a young man pushed his way past Manubehn, whipped out a pistol and fired three shots in quick succession. Gandhi tottered and fell instantly with the words *He Rama* (Oh God) on his lips. The apostle of non-violence died a martyr in the cause of love and brotherhood of man, at the hands of an assassin whose vision of brotherhood was too too narrow and tainted. Prime Minister Nehru, with his heart full of grief and a trembling voice choked with emotion, broke the tragic news to the nation, on the radio:

> The light has gone out of our lives and there is darkness everywhere and I do not quite know what to tell you and how to say it. Our beloved leader, Bapu as we call him, the father of our nation is no more. Perhaps I am wrong to say that. Nevertheless we will not see him again as we have seen him these many years.
>
>   The light has gone out, I said, and yet I was wrong. For the light that shone in this country was no ordinary light. The light that has illumined this country for these many years will illumine this country for many more years, and a thousand years later that light will be seen in this country, and the world will see it and it will give solace to innumerable hearts. For that light represented the living truth, and the eternal man was with us with

50   "The light has gone out of our lives"

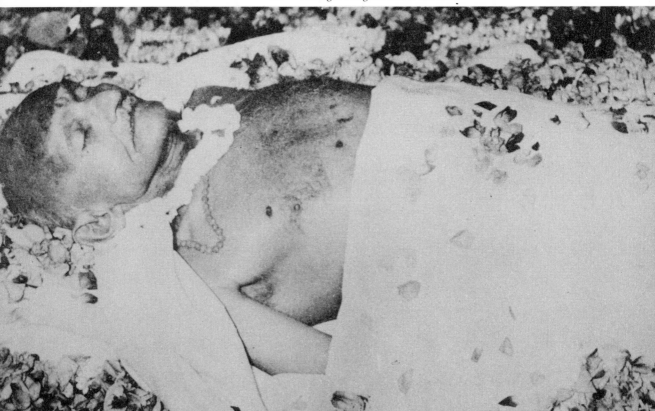

F L A SH.

DELHI NUMBER 25.   (GEN--XX).   NEW DELHI, JAN 30.

   MAHATMA GANDHI WAS SHOT AT THREE TIMES THIS EVENING

A P I. 30/1.CR.•5-30PM.PLEASE ACK IMMLY.'

7K

DELHI NUMBER 26.   F L A S H.   (SECOND FLASH).

   WORST IS FEARED.--A P I. 30/1.CR. 5- 30PM.

PLEASE ACK'.

F L A S H.

DELHI NUMBER 27.   (GEN--XX).   NEW DELHI,JAN 30.

   MAHTAMA GANDHI WAS SHOT AT FOUR TIMES WHILE HE WAS

WALKING TO THE PRAYER GROUND. HE IS SERIOUSLY INJURED.

  -A P I.30/1.CR. 5-40PM.PLEASE ACK '.

DELHI NUMBER 27.   (THIRD FLASH).

   DOCTORS HAVE BEEN SUMMONED. (MORE).-API . 30/1 .CR.

5-4PM.

52   Dr Rajendra Prasad
(later India's first
President) and V.
Patel (the Deputy
Prime Minister) pay
homage

his eternal truth reminding us of the right path, drawing us from error, taking this ancient country to freedom.

There is so much more to do. There was so much more for him to do.'

Mahatma Gandhi's assassination sent shock-waves throughout the world. Messages of condolence and appreciation of his selfless and priceless service to India and the world at large poured in from all quarters of the globe. Messages streamed in from the Pope, the King and Queen of England, President Truman, Mrs Roosevelt, the Archbishop of Canterbury, the Dalai Lama, Albert Einstein, the President of France, Leon Blum, General MacArthur and many other heads of state and countless other politicians, journalists and Indians from all walks of life. Extracts from some of these messages are reproduced below:

Rt Hon Clement Attlee
Everyone will have learnt with profound horror of the brutal murder of Mr Gandhi. I know that I am expressing the views of the British people in offering to his fellow countrymen our deep sympathy in the loss of their greatest citizen. Mahatma Gandhi, as he was known in India, was one of the outstanding figures in the world today, but he seemed to belong to a different period of history. Living a life of extreme asceticism, he was revered as a divinely inspired saint by millions of his fellow countrymen.

President Truman
Gandhi was a great Indian nationalist, but at the same time he was a leader of international stature. His teachings and his actions have left a deep impression on millions of people. . . .

Another giant among men has fallen in the cause of brotherhood and peace.

Mr Eamon De Valera
In its later phases our own struggle for freedom and that of India have coincided. Our people felt they were brothers in a common cause and wished each other

well. . . . The loss is not India's alone. The world has lost a great leader, whose influence will long survive after his death.

Sir M. Zafrulla Khan
His tragic death constitutes as grievous a loss to Pakistan as to India. It is an irreparable loss to the cause of peace throughout the world.

Pandit Jawaharlal Nehru: Tribute in Parliament, 2nd February 1948
We praise people in well-chosen words, and we have some kind of measure for greatness. How shall we praise him and how shall we measure him? For he was not of the common clay of which all of us are made. No words of praise of ours in this House are needed, for he has had greater praise in his life than any living man. In his history and during these two or three days since his death, he has had the homage of the world. What can we add to that?

. . . He has gone, and all over India there is a feeling of having been left desolate and forlorn . . . yet together with that feeling there is also a feeling of proud thanksgiving that it has been given to us of this generation to be associated with this mighty person in ages to come. Centuries, and it may be milleniums after us, people will think of this generation when this man of God trod the earth. They will think of us who, however small, could also follow his path, and they will probably tread on that holy ground where his feet had been. Let us be worthy of him. Let us always be so.

Earl Mountbatten of Burma
The Governor-General, Lord Mountbatten, broadcasting from New Delhi on 12th February said that the death of Mahatma Gandhi came with a shock of personal bereavement to millions of people in every part of the civilized world.

Not only those who worked with him throughout his life, or who, like myself, had known him for a comparatively short time, but people who had never met him, who had never seen him or had even read one word of his published works, felt as if they had lost a friend. . . . Gandhiji will have rendered his last and greatest service of all to the people he loved so well if the tragic manner of his death has shocked and spurred us into sinking all differences and joining in a sustained united effort – beginning here and now. Only in this way can this ideal be realized and India enter into her full inheritance.

General Douglas MacArthur
Nothing more revolting has occurred in the history of the modern world than the senseless assassination of this venerable man. He had come through time and circumstances and his oft-repeated ideologies are to be regarded as the very symbol and apotheosis of peace.

New York Times
A light has gone out. The rest remains for history's inexorable hand to write down. . . . His undying spirit speaks now to all India and the world. He has left as

53 Last journey to Rajghat (*overleaf*)

his spiritual heritage a spiritual force that must in God's good time prevail over armaments and dark doctrines.

Rt Hon Sir Stafford Cripps

The assassination of Mahatma Gandhi is a tragedy of the deepest intensity for India and the world. To his friends the loss will be even greater. His faith in non-violence was expressed not only in words but in his actions and in the self-sacrifice which he showed throughout his life.

There has been no greater spiritual leader in the world in our time. His loss will mean a setback and discouragement for those who, like him, believe above all in the spiritual values.

Louis Fischer

I had seen Gandhi, eaten with him, walked with him, talked with him, joked with him. I counted as golden the hours he gave me. Now reading the accounts of how the three bullets pierced his body and how he lay helpless before death, I wept though I had not wept for many years, and felt numb. Later, when I could think again, it seemed that maybe this was the best way to die. He was a fighter all his life, and it would have been strange if he had died of a cold. His violent death was one more service.

Gandhi is India's gift to the Western world; his life contains a prescription for some of our worst ills.

Manchester Guardian: 31st January 1948

A leader who shows perfect courage, perfect honesty, and absolute freedom from envy, hatred, malice, and all uncharitableness does not live in vain. To India, Mr Gandhi gave a new standard of courage and virtue in public life. To the West he is the man who revived and refreshed our sense of the meaning and value of religion.

M Georges Bidault

The world has heard today one of the saddest tidings of our time. He, who only a few days ago showed that good-will and renunciation would conquer hate and ambition, has left us, struck down by a madman. Not only his own people will mourn him, but all those who believe in the possibility of brotherly understanding. Mr Gandhi gave the example of an obstinate, and absolute search for love of mankind, whatever their race or religion. France stands tonight at the bier of this great man, fallen victim to the violence against which he always fought. May the sacrifice crown his life work.

Leon Blum

I never saw Gandhi. I do not know his language. I never set foot in his country, and yet I feel the same sorrow as if I had lost someone near and dear. The whole world has been plunged into mourning by the death of this extraordinary man.

Pearl Buck

Another Crucifixion.

Mr Horace Alexander, Society of Friends

The long struggle against British power never led to alienation from English people. . . . In the course of Gandhi's long life, many English men and women have been privileged to count themselves among his host of friends from the early days in South Africa, when Henry Polak and others supported the Satyagraha movement. On through the long years of his intimate friendship with C. F. Andrews, and right to the end of his life, he was surrounded by English friends.

Hearst Press USA

The assassination of Gandhi has had an emotional impact upon the world today that has no parallel in human history since the similar martyrdom of Lincoln, and it menaces the peace of the world today in a manner probably not equalled by any act of violence against any man since the assassination of Sarajevo.

Gandhi was not simply a great man, but a good man and as sorrowing people of many nations will know, the combination of the qualities of greatness and goodness in man is too rarely achieved and too little appreciated.

It is only the life of Gandhi which is at an end, for there is no work of destruction which could be wrought against the edifice of kindness and dignity, reason and justice, which he patiently and selflessly erected for the good of India and the peace of the world hour upon hour and day upon day and year upon year throughout the prolific time of his fruitful life.

Dr John Hayes Holmes: Memorial Service, Community Service Church, New York City, 1st February 1948

When all the kings and princes and great captains of our time, who make so much noise and occupy so central a place upon the stage, when these have long since been forgotten, every one of them, the Mahatma will still be known and revered as the greatest Indian since Gautama the Buddha, and as the greatest man since Jesus Christ.

Gandhi gave to the Indian people the weapons wherewith to carry on their fight, weapons of unimaginable power, weapons that guaranteed eventual victory, and in Gandhi's own time, praise be to God, won the victory that he could see. Gandhi's programme of non-violent resistance is unprecedented in the history of mankind. . . .

Moustapha El Nahas

The assassination of the great spiritual leader Mahatma Gandhi has deeply affected my friends and myself as it has the people of the Nile Valley. The death of the man of love and peace at the hands of a dastardly murderer adds to our affliction and bereavement and the great loss incurred by his disappearance is not limited to India and the East alone, but is felt in every corner of the world, for in truth he belonged to all mankind.

Rt Hon Philip Noel-Baker

This tragic event has taken from us a man venerated not only in his own country but by men of all the world.

Mr Gandhi was a man whose greatness belonged not only to his lifetime but to history. For half a century his inspiration has been unfailing, and in the past year, it perhaps attained its supreme expression . . . I believe that like other prophets his greatest work is still to come.

Rt Hon Lord Pethick-Lawrence

We must do homage by deeds. Gandhiji was deeply loved. He will be deeply mourned. He is no longer with us in flesh and blood, but his spirit endures. What was the secret of his power over the hearts and minds of men? In my opinion it was the fact that he voluntarily stripped himself of every vestige of the privilege that he could have enjoyed on account of his birth, means, personality, intellectual pre-eminence and took on himself the status and infirmities of the ordinary man.

Mr Fernand Van Langenhove: Security Council

A tragic event dominates our thoughts. We have met today [in the Security Council] under the spell of emotion which has gone through the world at the death of Mr Gandhi. . . . Mr Gandhi gave to the world a great lesson. . . . From the distance he appeared to us to be already above this world as a great symbol. . . . He lived long enough to see India become fully sovereign. But he represented something more – the idea of non-violence.

Rajkumari Amrit Kaur

In the twinkling of an eye, our greatest and most beloved leader, our friend, philosopher and guide, was taken away from us. More than leader, he was a father to us all. Not for nothing did we call him "Bapu". And we are today orphans. The fury of a madman has taken his frail body from our midst, but who can kill his spirit? He can never die, and we shall continue always to feel his presence near us and we shall, I hope be truer to him now than when he was with us.

He has won the martyr's crown. His soul is at rest. But he had to offer the supreme sacrifice for us. Let us not forget our guilt. Every true Indian must hang his head in utter shame that one of our own had fallen so low as to put an end to his precious life. May God forgive him, and may we try to forgive the assassin, as surely Bapu must have forgiven him and loved him even as he was firing at him.

George C. Marshall

Mahatma Gandhi was the spokesman for the conscience of mankind.

Most of these messages were published in Appendix II of *Mahatma Gandhi, Essays and Reflections on his Life and Work*, edited by the late Dr S. Radhakrishnan and published by George Allen and Unwin Ltd, London 1949. They are reproduced here by their kind permission.

54 The Gandhi *samadhi* (shrine) at Rajghat

Chapter 9
No Ordinary Light:
—⊷ The Mahatma's Influence ⊶—

THE LIGHT THAT had shone in India and the world during the first half of the twentieth century was no ordinary light, as stated by Nehru in his grief-stricken effusion on All-India Radio on the evening of Mahatma Gandhi's assassination. Mahatma Gandhi had made a unique impact on political and social developments during his lifetime and the glorious example of his own life and his teachings continue to inspire and influence millions in his own country and many others in different corners of the world. His campaign in South Africa for the removal of racial inequalities and the redress of the indignities heaped upon citizens of Indian origin, brought hope and encouragement to oppressed minorities in many lands. Gandhi's application of the weapon of satyagraha and non-violence in the struggle in South Africa and its extension on a massive scale to the freedom struggle in India infused a new spirit of self-confidence and faith in their own strength amongst millions of subjugated people all over the world. Indian independence lit the fuse that set the pace for the dissolution of the British Empire and the retreat of imperialism from over sixty countries within a matter of two decades after the independence of India.

Gandhi was the leader of the challenge to Western domination and while his actions on the political scene changed the face of the map, he was a man of all seasons: a statesman, a politician, a social reformer, a man of religion, a humanitarian, an educator, an economist, a revolutionary and a dreamer, a dietician and nature-cure faddist, all rolled in one. He was a rational man but did not fit any particular label – conservative, anarchist, liberal, radical, socialist or communist. There are few aspects of life which escaped his attention and he made his own assessments on life's problems, in the light of his basic principles and his experiments with truth. "To him life was an integrated whole, a closely woven garment of many colours, a word to a child, a touch of healing to the sufferer was as important as a resolution of challenge to the British Empire. He was a complete man."★

Many significant changes have taken place in the world since Gandhi's death. Many national heroes, contemporaries of Gandhi – Lenin, Stalin, Hitler, Mussolini, Mao and Churchill have played their part and left the stage. We live in a more violent world today. The world is sharply divided by problems of racial strife, the North-South

★ Government of India: *The Collected Works of Mahatma Gandhi*, Volume I, Foreword

101

divide and East-West tensions. Gandhi had given thought to these problems and challenges which have bedevilled humanity for many years, and suggested remedies, based on tolerance, love, understanding and non-violence. But Gandhi was no armchair strategist or impractical visionary. He analysed the causes of war and suggested ways of dealing with them. According to him, the major intractable problems in international relations were the result of western imperialism, fascism, and communism. He suggested economic justice, sovereign equality and peaceful co-operation as the remedies for political and economic rivalries. Economic imperialism and racial conflict still remain as major causes of international tensions. Gandhi was in favour of unilateral disarmament and the use of third party settlement for resolving international disputes. He advocated World Government and conceded the need for the establishment of an international police force, but was totally against the maintenance of war machines by individual states – he recommended satyagraha as a substitute for military action. Gandhi also held that human beings belonged to one large family in spite of their differences in sex, colour and race. He believed in perfect equality between man and man.

Gandhi had once said "the atomic bomb has deadened the finest feelings that have sustained mankind for ages" and "behind the death-dealing bomb there is the human hand that releases it, and behind that still, is the human heart that sets the hand in motion." Pyare Lal, Mahatma Gandhi's secretary, analyses and discusses the implications of this psychic phenomenon, in his book, *Last Phase*:

> The final battle for the survival of civilisation and perhaps of the human race itself has thus to be fought in the psyche of man, which is in Jung's words "in the last resort . . . the place of origin of all action, and therefore everything which happens by the will of man." If we could control the psyche of the individual, who manipulates atomic power, it should give us the power to control the diabolical power which the run-away science of man threatens to unleash.★

Mahatma Gandhi's original and most remarkable contribution to the world has been the technique of non-violent resistance in place of violence for the resolution of social and political conflicts. His message of love and non-violence has a universal appeal and it has been adopted by many peace, protest, resistance movements and freedom campaigns, in many countries outside India with varying degrees of success. The concept of non-violence was not new, but its use was mostly confined to non-violent protests by individuals. Gandhi's unique contribution consists in perfecting it as a technique for group protests and the substitution of love in place of hate as its motivating force and strength. Gandhi's ideas on satyagraha, which were derived from his own Hindu heritage, were reinforced by his study of Tolstoy and Thoreau and according to Pyare Lal:

> Gandhiji's contribution consisted in forging out of it a sanction for society, for the solution of world problems and bringing to bear on the investigation of its techniques, patient experimental accuracy and the critical detachment of a modern scientist. . . . A couple of months before his death, Tolstoy in a letter to Gandhiji predicted that the non-violent work

★ Pyare Lal: *Mahatma Gandhi – The Last Phase*, Part II, Navajivan Publishing House, Ahmedabad, 1958.

that he, Gandhiji, was engaged in in South Africa was the one in which the whole of the Christian and non-Christian world was bound one day to participate.★

Gandhi had stated once that the science of satyagraha was "science in the making". He was, however, confident about further discoveries in the field: "We are constantly being astonished these days at the amazing discoveries in the field of violence. But I maintain that far more undreamt of and seemingly impossible discoveries will be made in the field of non-violence." Pyare Lal concludes:

> The weapon of non-violent resistance or soul-force which Gandhiji has given to the world is thus the fruit and culmination of the researches of savants from all over the world. It is the common heritage of all the down-trodden and oppressed people of the earth in the battle of right against wrong, of freedom and justice against tyranny, of the spirit against the power of armaments, and if one might say so, their only hope.
>
> We hear so much these days of international control and development of international control and development of atomic energy. Cannot there be international co-operation for the development and use of this unique power about which Jung, that greatest of living psychologists, has testified: "Psychic life is a world power that excels by many times all the powers of the earth."★

In the land of his birth the Mahatma is a living presence. He was able to unite the people of India, restore their sense of self-respect and prestige and release their energies in the cause of the nation's political struggle and social reform. Those who were cynical about the awakening of the Indian masses, who were held to be far too passive and fatalistic in their attitude to function as effective freedom fighters were amazed. Under Gandhi's moral and spiritual and political leadership, the masses arose from their deep slumber and showed themselves capable of enormous strength, courage and a capacity to endure hardships, so essential for a successful non-violent campaign. They gave evidence of unpredictable reserves of hidden power and responded to his call for active participation in constructive work in the villages. In response to the Mahatma's call, professional classes, including academics, lawyers, doctors, members of the business community gave up their professional careers and business interests and flocked to Gandhi to render service to the country. Gandhi was a shrewd judge of men and was able to attract brilliant Indians from all walks of life who became his trusted lieutenants. He was humble and had a great gift for reconciling opposites and was thus able to win the confidence and affections of leaders who were so different from him in their views and their temperaments. Jawaharlal Nehru and Sardar Vallabhbhai Patel, diametrically opposed to each other in approach and temperament were able to work together because of their deference to Gandhi's wishes. Gandhi stirred the whole country out of its depths and the people of India gave him their unqualified love and adulation. Gandhi's conquests of the hearts of men were based on *ahimsa* and love. There is hardly any field, political, educational, economic, the uplift of Harijans, emancipation of women, rural uplift by cottage industries and spiritual regeneration, which he ignored and did not transform by his magic touch. Since his death, his influence has been mostly in the field of social, educational and

★ Pyare Lal: *The Last Phase*

constructive work, although the mechanism of the state has not been able to implement Gandhi's ideas on disarmament and the setting up of self-sufficient village republics.

The Mahatma is also an unforgettable presence, wherever you are in India, and there is no dearth of visible reminders of the man. Streets, public buildings, parks and squares, hospitals, social, educational and welfare institutions, housing colonies and in fact whole cities bear witness to his name and fame. Statues in stone and bronze, portraits and pictures depicting the life of the Mahatma are in evidence everywhere. Even the commercial artists churning out cheap imitations thrive on the feelings of great reverence for Gandhi and do a roaring trade.

Gandhi's birthplace, all the places associated with the Mahatma's earthly sojourn, in fact every inch of ground where he trod or stopped for a while have become hallowed spots. Rajghat, the site in Delhi where he was cremated has become a shrine and a national monument. The place is a focus for visitors; Heads of State, foreign dignitaries and thousands upon thousands of his countrymen, flock from near and far to pay homage to their departed "Bapu". His scanty material possessions are on public display in museums and the Gandhi ashrams.

Gandhi had considerable personal magnetism and a unique capacity for making friends. During his long life, he attracted a large circle of Englishmen and women as friends, fellow-pilgrims and disciples. The political struggle for independence did not stand in the way of his making friends with all he came across. He delighted in

55 Mani Bhavan, where Gandhi lived and worked while in Bombay, now holds one of the finest collections of his books and photographs

their friendship and kept up voluminous correspondence with them on an amazing diversity of themes ranging from personal trivia to his philosophical concepts.

Every word uttered by Gandhi in his speeches and conversations, his prolific output as a journalist, his voluminous correspondence, covering a period of almost the first half of this century, is published in the *Collected Works of Mahatma Gandhi*. This monumental collection runs to over 85 volumes of about 550 pages each. Gandhi had a flair for writing and he edited and profusely contributed to the journal *Indian Opinion*, founded by him in South Africa, and to *Young India* and *Harijan* in India. His contributions were on a tremendous range of subjects, from dieting and nature cures to complex political, social and religious issues.

Departments of Gandhian Philosophy in Universities, Institutes of Gandhian studies and other organizations devoted to the implementation of Gandhian constructive programmes are engaged in useful work. Gandhi Memorial Lectures are held on a regular basis in many centres. Gandhi ashrams provide opportunities for practical work and experience in an environment based on simple living and high thinking. The most notable among the institutions devoted to implementation of Gandhi's work on the practical plane is the Gandhi Peace Foundation. It has a network of several branches throughout the country and carries out research into peace activities and Gandhian philosophy, sponsors lectures, seminars and workshops and publishes a newsletter. It also publishes a monthly journal *Gandhi Marg* (The Path of Gandhi), a renowned journal, which enjoys wide popularity in academic, professional, and research circles in India and the world at large.

Vinoba Bhave, his devoted disciple, who joined Gandhi's ashram in Ahmedabad (Sabarmati) in 1916 carried on Mahatma Gandhi's social and constructive programme for many years after Gandhi's death. He walked from village to village, and demanded gifts of land from the better-off land owning families for the landless. The saintly personality of Vinoba, in the very image of Gandhi, was met with generous response and respect. Vinoba is now very old and feeble but his work is carried out by a team of dedicated volunteers. Jai Prakash Narayan, the veteran socialist leader, who could have become India's next Prime Minister, after Nehru, joined ranks with Vinoba and carried on his *Bhoodan* work, along with *Sarvodaya* (welfare of all). With the retirement of Vinoba Bhave and the death of J.P. the work continues, carried on by hundreds of dedicated and selfless volunteers and social workers.

Modern India, the heir to the spiritual legacy of Mahatma Gandhi has adopted some of the elements of Gandhi's constructive programmes with partial success. The Cottage Industries programme has been adopted by the State Government and there has been appreciable expansion in this sector. Untouchability has been abolished by law and the position of Harijans is substantially better. The battle for the hearts has, however, still to be won and the country has a long way to go yet. Women's rights have been enshrined in the Constitution of India, and they are gradually marching shoulder to shoulder with their men. Many social and evil practices affecting their status and treatment still remain to be rescinded. Gandhi's concern for the rights of the individual and faith in democracy has been vindicated.

India has made efforts to wean itself away from reliance on force for the settlement of international disputes. It has not however been able to set an example to the rest of the world by adoption of unilateral disarmament in accordance with Gandhi's wishes.

Gandhi's message went beyond India's shores to the black people in Africa and the U.S.A. Ali Mazrui states that

> In Africa, the Gandhian torch passed to Kwame Nkrumah, the leader at that time of Gold Coast nationalism. In June 1949, Nkrumah launched the strategy of "Positive Action" as a form of harassing British authorities to grant one concession after another to the nationalist movement. In his autobiography Nkrumah tells how he explained the strategy to a critical traditional local council. "I described Positive Action as the adoption of all legitimate and constitutional means by which we could attack the forces of imperialism in the country. The weapons were legitimate political agitation, newspaper and educational campaigns and, as a last resort the constitutional application of strikes, boycotts and non-cooperation based on the principle of absolute non-violence, as used by Gandhi in India." With the launching of "Positive Action", Nkrumah earned the name not only of "Apostle of Freedom" but also of "Gandhi of Ghana". Years later, Nkrumah was to say: "we salute Mahatma Gandhi and we remember in tribute to him, that it was in South Africa that this method of non-violence and non-cooperation was first practised."*

Gandhiism had penetrated West Africa by the 1920s, when the West African Congress was established, inspired as it was by the news about the existence of the Indian National Congress in India. During these years, West Africans were impressed by the unity in the Congress in India. A pioneer nationalist paper in Nigeria, *Lagos Weekly Record* had observed "we hope the day will come soon when. . . . Hausas, Yorubas, and Ibos will make a common stand and work hand in hand with their fatherland." By 1947, with the emergence of Pakistan, Nigerian leaders were becoming apprehensive about the possible repercussions of dissension and the Indian experience was being looked upon as a danger signal to states wishing to preserve their unity. Ali Mazrui writes that in some ways Mahatma Gandhi had become a political

* Ali A. Mazrui: *Political Values and the Educated Class in Africa*, Heinemann Educational Books, London.

56   Kenneth Kaunda of Zambia

antidote to Jesus Christ in Africa, because the message of Jesus had been used to encourage submission from the natives. Gandhi offered the element of resistance "added to the passivity of imperial christianity." Gandhi's views on rural development and decentralization have evoked a sympathetic response in many countries in the Third World and in Africa. The concept of "Ujamma" villages in Tanzania, introduced by Mwalimu (teacher) Julius Nyerere, who is a true Gandhian in spirit, is something that would have gladdened Gandhi's heart. President Kaunda of Zambia has been a lifelong admirer of Gandhi. He says in *Light from the East*

> If I owe my faith to Jesus, Mahatma Gandhi supplied the hope. His teachings flooded my mind with light brightening those corners, where I stored perplexing questions, I had gnawed on for years without result. . . . To someone like myself in such straits buffetted by events, inwardly torn by moral dilemmas, Gandhi's concept of satyagraha, the creative use of non-violent resistance as a strategy for change was a life-belt thrust into the hands of a drowning man.★

Gandhian inspired non-violent techniques were also used in certain Nazi-occupied countries, in Norway and Denmark in 1944, with some success.

Arnold Toynbee, the eminent British historian had once observed that "Gandhi was as great a benefactor of my country as his own. Gandhi made it impossible for the British to go on ruling India, but at the same time he made it possible for us to abdicate without rancour and dishonour". During the uneasy years, when the Indian Freedom Struggle subjected British political circles to considerable pressure, Gandhi was considered devious, unreliable and a troublemaker. Churchill described him as a "half-naked fakir". Although Gandhi spent several years in imprisonment, he maintained his belief in British decency and entertained the hope that the better conscience would one day wake up. In 1920, the Mahatma wrote: "Even under the most adverse circumstances, I have found Englishmen amenable to reason and persuasion and, as they always wish to appear just, it is easier to shame them into doing the right thing." Again a letter to the Viceroy, Lord Irwin, in 1930 before embarking on the famous Dandi March, the Mahatma expressed his friendship for the British, "though I hold the British rule in India to be a curse, I do not therefore consider Englishmen in general to be worse than any other people on earth. I have the privilege of claiming many Englishmen as dearest friends."

Among these friends, Gandhi counted several British politicians, governors and Viceroys, including Lord Irwin (later Lord Halifax), Lord Pethick-Lawrence, Sir Stafford Cripps, Lord Noel-Baker and Lord Fenner Brockway, many of whom had lobbied for the independence of India.

Gandhi's concept of non-violence continues to inspire several protest and peace movements in Britain: the Peace Pledge Union and War Resisters International, with its headquarters in London, who study Gandhian ideas and techniques of satyagraha. Some of the techniques employed by the Campaign for Nuclear Disarmament and the Labour Movement in the country bear close resemblance to the techniques em-

★ Kenneth David Kaunda: *Kaunda on Violence*, Sphere, London, 1980

ployed by Gandhi during the Indian freedom struggle. Seminars on Gandhian thought and non-violence are held from time to time and being attended by an increasing number of young people dedicated to the abolition of war and the winning of enduring peace.

American awareness of Gandhi came about in a rather unusual manner. John Hayes Holmes, a prominent Unitarian minister and reformer, who had been a pacifist during World War I, came across an article about Gandhi's non-violent campaign in South Africa in 1910 and instantly fell under his spell. Holmes, who had never even heard of Gandhi's name, was mesmerized, "he was everything I believed but hardly dared to hope. He was a dream come true." He hailed this revelation in a sermon "The Christ of Today" in 1921 and this was followed by another sermon with the title "Who is the Greatest Man in the World today?" This description and comparison with Christ intrigued Americans who had not come across this kind of un-American name until then. Subsequently Holmes also serialized Gandhi's autobiography in his magazine, *Unity*.

American interest in Gandhi had been aroused. Romain Rolland's excellent biographical study of Gandhi and the three volumes by C.F. Andrews were bringing Gandhi into the limelight. Newspapers and journals like *World Tomorrow, Current History* and the *New York Times* carried regular articles on Gandhi and the Freedom Struggle of India. *Catholic World* and *Christian Century* focused attention on the Gandhian concepts of "truth" and "non-violence". Lecture tours by Gandhi's English friends, Muriel Lester, Charlie Andrews and others served to highlight the national struggle in India and whip up American support. John Gunther's sympathetic accounts of Gandhi and Nehru, together with Louis Fischer and others kept interest centred on India. Groups of Americans began to identify themselves with the struggle against imperialism and some sections were amused and even delighted by the attempts to twist the tail of the British lion.

American public opinion was being courted by both Gandhi's friends and by the British who were not too happy about Americans getting too deeply concerned or embroiled in Indian politics. An American League for Indian Independence was formed in 1932. The Salt March and Gandhi's threatened death fast were reported widely. *The Christian Century* went to the extent of drawing parallels between Gandhi's fast to death and the crucifixion of Christ and when the Atlantic Charter was published in August 1941, leaders of the Indian National Congress took the opportunity to raise the question of Indian independence. In a letter to President Roosevelt, Gandhi stated, "I venture to think that the allies' fight to make the world safe for freedom of the individual and for democracy sounds hollow so long as India and for that matter Africa are exploited by Great Britain."

American liberal organizations and the press were disappointed when Churchill announced on 9th September that the Atlantic Charter did not apply to the British Empire. *Life* magazine published an open letter from the editors to the people of England, which assured them of American support but added:

The Americans may have some disagreement among ourselves as to what we are fighting for, but one thing we are sure, what we are not fighting for is to hold the British Empire together. We don't want to put the matter so bluntly, but we do not want you to have any illusions. We realize that you have a difficult problem in India, but we do not see that your "solution" to date provides any evidence of principles of any kind. In the light of what you are doing in India, how do you expect us to talk about "Principles" and look our soldiers in the eye.

Slavery was abolished in USA on 1st January 1863. By the turn of the twentieth century, however, Jim Crow laws and segregation in southern American society had reduced the negroes to second class citizens. Many organizations had been formed towards the beginning of the twentieth century to advocate the cause of these oppressed minorities and by the 1930s, Gandhian techniques of non-violence had begun to attract Negro ministers involved in the struggle for racial equality and justice. When Benjamin Mays and Howard Thurman went to India to meet Gandhi and to seek his advice Gandhi recommended the use of non-violent techniques and commented "It may be through the Negroes that the unadulterated message of non-violence will be delivered to the world." The American Friends Society invited Indian speakers to explain and elucidate Gandhian campaigns in India. The World Peace Movement held

57   Gandhi's statue in Tavistock Square, London, unveiled by the Prime Minister, Harold Wilson, in 1968

its meeting in India in 1949 and discussed how Gandhian ideas could be applied in their own struggle and satyagraha entered the American political consciousness, and became a living force with the publication of several brilliant analyses of the philosophy of non-violence by leading American thinkers, philosophers, historians and theorists. Notable among these were Richard Gregg's *The Power of Non-Violence* which became a bible for non-violent protesters, Vincent Sheean's *Lead, Kindly Light*, a book of considerable literary excellence, John S. Hoyland's *The Cross Moves East*, Krishan Lal Shridharni's *War, Without Violence* and more recently Joan V. Bondurant's remarkable book *Conquest of Violence: The Gandhian Philosophy of Conflict*, which is one of the best scientific interpretations of the subject. Professor Erik Erikson's *Gandhi's Truth* was awarded the Pullitzer Prize. More scientific studies of non-violence have been published in the United States than in any other country of the world, barring India.

Although interest in Gandhian techniques had been gaining ground for a number of years, it needed the dynamic personality of Martin Luther King to give it a practical shape in the American Civil Rights campaign in the 1950s. Dr King discovered Gandhi during a talk in Philadelphia by Dr M. Johnson, the president of Howard University, on the life and thought of Gandhi. King was highly moved. Writing about it a few years later, he said

> His message was so profound and electrifying that I left the meeting and bought half-a-dozen books on Gandhi's life and works. . . . As I read I became fascinated by his campaigns of non-violent resistance . . .[*]

That was a turning point in King's life and he confides:

> Gandhian concept of satyagraha was profoundly significant to me. As I delved deeper into the philosophy of Gandhi, my scepticism concerning the power of love gradually diminished, and I came to see for the first time that the Christian doctrine of love, operating through the Gandhian method of non-violence, is one of the most potent weapons available to an oppressed people in the struggle for their freedom.[*]

The fusion of Christian doctrine and Gandhian techniques was adopted as the guiding principle of the Civil Rights Movement and Martin Luther King demonstrated as no one had done before, how satyagraha, which germinated on South African soil and was nourished in India, had universal application. King used the power of the new technique to great effect in the boycott of city buses by the Negro community in Montgomery, Alabama. It unified the Negro community, and welded them together into a powerful force, fully conscious of their rights. The experience in Montgomery reinforced his belief in non-violence and he did not waver in his faith until his dying day. "The experience of Montgomery did more to clarify my thinking in regard to the question of non-violence than all the books that I had read. I became more and more convinced of the power of non-violence."

Montgomery was followed by the Birmingham protest against segregation, in 1963. The authorities clamped him in jail. Here he wrote "the letter from Birmingham Jail", which has been called the most incisive and eloquent statement of his racial

[*]   Lerone Bennet Jr.: *What Manner of Man,* Johnson Publishing Co, Chicago.

philosophy. In this letter he answered eight white clergymen who denounced him:

> I am in Birmingham because injustice is here. Gandhi has said "so long as the superstition that men should obey unjust laws exists, so long will their slavery exist." . . . any law that uplifts human personality is just. Any law that degrades human personality is unjust. All segregation statutes are unjust because segregation distorts the soul and damages the personality.

In the summer of 1963, King was ready to march on Washington. It was to be the occasion of his memorable speech, "I have a dream . . .".

In 1964, Martin Luther King was awarded the Nobel Prize for Peace. During his acceptance speech, he said "after contemplation, I conclude that this award which I receive . . . is a profound recognition that non-violence is the answer to the crucial political and moral question of our time: the need for man to overcome oppression and violence without resorting to violence and oppression. Civilization and violence are antithetical concepts. Negroes of the U.S. following the people of India have demonstrated that non-violence is not sterile passivity, but a powerful and moral force which makes for social transformation. I accept this award today with an abiding faith in America and an audacious faith in the future for mankind . . . I refuse the cynical notion that nation after nation must spiral down a militaristic stairway into the hall of the nuclear destruction. I believe that unarmed truth and unconditional love will have the final word in reality. I still believe that we shall overcome."

58 Dr Martin Luther King receives the Nobel Peace Prize, 1964

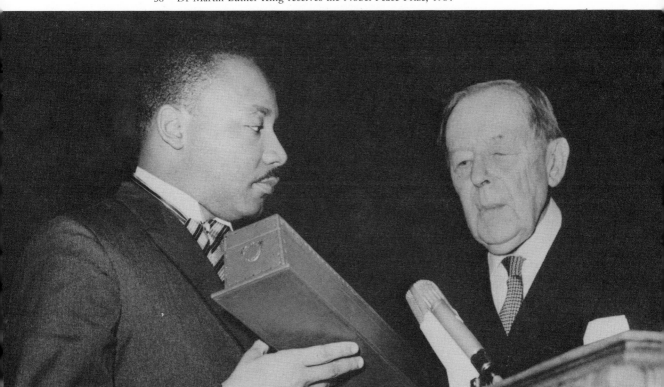

Chapter 10
—◦→ In His Own Words ←◦—

I HAVE NOTHING new to teach the world. Truth and non-violence are as old as the hills. All I have done is to try experiments in both on as vast a scale as I could do. In doing so, I have sometimes erred and learnt by my errors. Life and its problems have thus become to me so many experiments in the practice of truth and non-violence. . . .

All my philosophy, if it may be called by that pretentious name, is contained in what I have said. But you will not call it "Gandhism"; there is no "ism" about it. And no elaborate literature or propaganda is needed about it. The scriptures have been quoted against my position, but I have held faster than ever to the position that truth may not be sacrificed for anything whatsoever. Those who believe in the simple truths I have laid down can propagate them only by living them.

An Average Man
I claim to be no more than an average man with less than average ability. Nor can I claim any special merit for such non-violence or continence as I have been able to reach with laborious research. I have not the shadow of a doubt that any man or woman can achieve what I have, if he or she would make the same effort and cultivate the same hope and faith.

I look upon myself as a dull person. I take more time than others in understanding some things, but I do not care. There is a limit to man's progress in intelligence; but the developments of the qualities of the heart knows no bounds. It is literally true in my case that God provides the man of faith with such intelligence as he needs. I have always honoured and reposed faith in elders and wise men. But my deepest faith is in truth so that my path though difficult to tread has seemed easy to me.

I deny being a visionary. I claim to be a practical idealist. I do not accept the claim of saintliness. I am of the earth, earthy . . . I am prone to as many weaknesses as you are. But I have seen the world. I have lived in the world with my eyes open. I have gone through the most fiery ordeals that have fallen to the lot of man. I have gone through this discipline.

Have a Heart
It is better in prayer to have a heart without words than words without a heart.

Humour

I have been known as a crank, faddist, madman. Evidently the reputation is well deserved. For wherever I go, I draw to myself cranks, faddists and madmen. If I had no sense of humour, I should long ago have committed suicide.

Belief in the Truth of all Religions and Respect for them

I disbelieve in the conversion of one person by another. My effort should never be to undermine another's faith but to make him a better follower of his own faith. This implies the belief in the truth of all religions and respect for them. It again implies true humility, a recognition of the fact that the divine light having been vouchsafed to all religions through an imperfect medium of flesh, they must share in more or less degree the imperfection of the vehicle.

Goodness and Knowledge

Goodness must be joined with knowledge. Mere goodness is not of much use. One must retain the fine discriminating quality which goes with spiritual courage and character. One must know in a critical situation when to speak and to be silent, when to act and when to refrain. Action and non-action in these circumstances become identical instead of being contradictory.

Anger

I have learnt through bitter experience the one supreme lesson to conserve my anger, and as heat conserved is transmuted into energy, even so our anger controlled can be transmuted into a power which can move the world.

Love

Love never claims, it ever gives. Love ever suffers, never resents, never revenges itself.

Hate

I hold myself to be incapable of hating any being on earth. By a long course of prayerful discipline, I have ceased . . . to hate anybody. I know this is a big claim. Nevertheless I make it in all humility.

But I can and do hate evil wherever it exists. I hate the system that the British people have set up in India. I hate the ruthless exploitation of India even as I hate from the bottom of my heart the hideous system of untouchability for which millions of Hindus have made themselves responsible. But I do not hate the domineering Englishman, as I refuse to hate the domineering Hindus. I seek to reform them in all the loving ways that are open to me. My non-cooperation has its roots not in hatred but in love.

On God

There is an indefinable mysterious power that pervades everything. I feel it, though I do not see it. It is this unseen power which makes itself felt and yet defies all proof, because it is so unlike all that I perceive through my senses. But it is possible to reason out God to a certain extent . . . there is an unalterable law governing everything or every being that exists or lives . . . That law, then, which governs all life is God. Law and the law-giver are one. I may not deny the law or the law-giver because I know so little about it or Him. Just as my denial or ignorance of the existence of an earthly power will avail me nothing, even so my denial of God will not liberate me from its operation: whereas humble and mute acceptance of divine authority makes life's journey easier even as the acceptance of earthly rule makes life under it easier.

God is not a person . . . He is the essence of life. He is pure and undefiled consciousness. To seek God one need not go on pilgrimage or light lamps and burn incense before or anoint the image of the deity or paint it with red vermilion. For He resides in our hearts. If we could completely obliterate in us the consciousness of our physical body, we would see Him face to face.

Different Abodes of God

Temples or mosques or churches . . . I make no distinction between these different abodes of God. They are what faith has made them. They are an answer to man's craving somehow to reach the unseen.

Violence

I object to violence because when it appears to do good, the good it does is temporary, the evil it does is permanent. I do not believe in violent short-cuts to success . . . however much I may sympathize and admire worthy motives. I am an uncompromising opponent of violent methods even to serve the noblest of causes . . . experience convinces me that permanent good can never be the outcome of untruth and violence.

Ahimsa *or the Way of Non-Violence*

Non-violence is the greatest force at the disposal of mankind. It is mightier than the mightiest weapon of destruction devised by the ingenuity of man. Destruction is not the law of the humans. Man lives freely by his readiness to die, if need be at the hands of his brother, never by killing him . . . just as one must learn the art of killing in the training for violence, so one must learn the art of dying in the training for non-violence . . . the votary of non-violence has to cultivate the capacity for sacrifice of the highest order to be free from fear . . . he who has not overcome all fear cannot practise *Ahimsa* to perfection.

Non-Violence and Cowardice

Non-violence and cowardice go ill together. I can imagine a fully armed man to be at heart a coward. Possession of arms implies an element of fear, if not cowardice. But true non-violence is an impossibility without the possession of unadulterated fearlessness.

He who takes to his heels the moment he sees two people fighting is not non-violent but a coward. A non-violent person will lay down his life in preventing such quarrels.

Satyagraha

A satyagrahi bids goodbye to fear. He is therefore never afraid of trusting the opponent . . . it is often forgotten that it is never the intention of a satyagrahi to embarrass the wrongdoer. He should avoid artificiality in all his doings. He acts naturally and from inward conviction.

Satyagraha is gentle. It never wounds. It must not be the result of anger or malice. It is never fussy, never impatient, never vociferous. It is the direct opposite of compulsion. It was conceived as a complete substitute for violence.

There is no time-limit for a satyagrahi nor is there a limit to his capacity for suffering . . . joy lies in the fight, in the attempt, in the suffering involved, not in the victory itself. Hence there is no such thing as defeat in satyagraha.

Means and Ends
Means and ends are convertible terms in my philosophy of life. They say "means are after all means", I would say means are after all everything. As the means so the end. There is no wall of separation between means and end. Indeed the creator has given us control over means, none over the end . . .

Message to a person who thought that any means could be justified for laudable ends:
Your belief that there is no connection between the means and the end is a great mistake. Through that mistake even men who have been considered religious have committed grievous crimes. Your reasoning is the same as saying that we can get a rose through planting a noxious weed . . . the means may be likened to a seed, the end to a tree; and there is just the same inviolable connection between the means and the end as there is between the seed and the tree. I am not likely to obtain the result from the worship of God by laying myself prostrate before Satan. If, therefore, anyone were to say: "I want to worship God; it does not matter that I do so by means of Satan", it would be set down as ignorant folly. We reap exactly as we sow.

Economics and Ethics
I must confess that I do not draw a sharp line or any distinction between economics and ethics. Economics that hurt the moral well-being of an individual or a nation are immoral and, therefore sinful. Thus, the economics that permit one country to prey upon another are immoral.

Individual Freedom
I value individual freedom but you must not forget that man is essentially a social being. He has risen to his present status by learning to adjust his individualism to the requirements of social progress. Unrestricted individualism is the law of the beast of the jungle. We have learnt to strike the mean between individual freedom and social restraint. Willing submission to social restraint for the sake of the well-being of the society enriches both the individual and the society of which one is a member.

Civil Disobedience
Civil disobedience is the inherent right of a citizen. He dare not give it up without ceasing to be a man. Civil disobedience is never followed by anarchy. Criminal disobedience can lead to it. Every state puts down criminal disobedience by force. It

perishes if it does not. But to put down civil disobedience is to attempt to imprison conscience.

Democracy
Democracy disciplined and enlightened is the finest thing in the world. A democracy prejudiced, ignorant, superstitious will land itself in chaos and may be self-destroyed.

On Education
By education I mean an all-round drawing out of the best in child and man – body, mind and spirit. But unless the development of the mind and body goes hand in hand with a corresponding awakening of the soul, the former alone would prove to be a lopsided affair. By spiritual training I mean education of the heart.

On Women
I am firmly of the opinion that India's salvation depends on the sacrifice and en-lightenment of her women . . . *Ahimsa* means infinite love, which again means infi-nite capacity for suffering. Who, but woman, the mother of man, shows this capacity in the largest measure? . . . If I were born a woman, I would rise in rebellion against any pretension on the part of man that woman is born to be his plaything. I have men-tally become a woman to steal into her heart. I could not steal into my wife's heart until I decided to treat her differently than I used to do, and so I restored to her all my so-called rights as her husband.

Brotherhood of Man
My mission is not merely brotherhood of Indian humanity. My mission is not merely freedom of India. But through realization of the freedom of India, I hope to realize and carry on the brotherhood of man.

Bibliography

Alexander, Horace G.: *India Since Cripps,* Penguin, London, 1944.
———: *Gandhi Through Western Eyes,* Asia Publishing House, London, 1969.
Andrews, C.F.: *Mahatma Gandhi's Ideas*, Allen and Unwin, London, 1929, and the Macmillan Company, New York, 1930.
———: *Mahatma Gandhi: His Own Story*, Allen and Unwin, London, 1930, and the Macmillan Company, New York, 1930.
———: *Mahtma Gandhi at Work* Allen and Unwin, London and the Macmillan Company, New York, 1931.
Ashe, Geoffrey: *Gandhi: A Study in Revolution*, Heinemann, London, 1968, and Stein and Day, New York, 1968.
Azad, Maulana A.K.: *India Wins Freedom*, Orient Longmans, Bombay, 1955.
Bernays, Robert: *Naked Fakir*, Victor Gollancz, London, 1931.
Bhattacharya, Bhabani C.: *Gandhi the Writer*, National Book Trust, New Delhi, 1969.
———: *Mahatma Gandhi*, Arnold-Heinemann, New Delhi, 1977.
Birla, G.D.: *In the Shadow of the Mahatma*, Orient Longmans Ltd, Bombay, 1953.
Black, Jo Anne: *Gandhi the Man,* Glide Publications, San Francisco, 1972.
Bondurant, Joan V.: *Conquest of Violence: The Gandhian Philosophy of Conflict*, Princeton University Press, Princeton, U.S.A., 1958.
Bose, Nirmal Kumar: *My Days with Gandhi*, Indian Associated Publishing Co, Calcutta, 1953.
———: *Gandhi in Indian Politics*, Lalvani Publishing House, Bombay, 1967.
Bourke-White, Margaret: *Half-way to Freedom*, Simon and Schuster, New York, 1949.
Brown, Judith M.: *Gandhi's Rise to Power*; Cambridge University Press, 1972.
Catlin, George: *In the Path of Mahatma Gandhi*, Macdonald & Co, London, 1948.
Chatfield, Charles, (Editor): *The Americanization of Mahatma Gandhi: Images of the Mahatma*, Garland Publishing Co Ltd, New York and London, 1976.
Datta, Dhirendra Mohan: *The Philosophy of Mahatma Gandhi*, University of Wisconsin Press, Madison, U.S.A., 1961.
Desai, Mahadev: *The Diaries*, Navajivan Publishing House, Ahmedabad, India, 1953.
———: *The Gospel of Selfless Action*, Navajivan, Ahmedabad, 1956.
Deshpande P.G. (Editor): *Gandhiana: A Bibliography of Gandhian Literature*, Navajivan, Ahmedabad, revised edition, 1948.
Doke, Joseph J.: *M. K. Gandhi*, G. A. Nateson & Co, Madras, 1909.
Fischer, Louis: *The Life of Mahatma Gandhi*, Harper and Brothers, New York, 1950, and Jonathan Cape, London, 1951.
———: *A Week with Gandhi*, Duell, Sloan and Pearce, New York, 1942.
Gandhi, Manubehn: *Bapu my Mother*, Navajivan, Ahmedabad, 1962.
Gandhi, Mohandas Karamchand: *Satyagraha in South Africa*, G. A. Nateson, Madras, 1928; *Hind Swaraj*, 1938; *Constructive Programme*, 1941; *Economics of Khadi*, 1941; *My Appeal to the British*, John Day Co, New York, 1942; *The Story of My Experiments with Truth*, Navajivan, 1945, Public Affairs Press, Washington, 1948 and Beacon Press, Boston, 1957; *India of my Dreams*, 1947; *Sarvodaya*, 1951; *Untouchability*, 1954; *The Collected Works of Mahatma Gandhi*, Publications Division, Government of India, New Delhi, 1958-(still being published); *Selected Letters*, 1962; *Nature Cure*, 1964.
Note: Except where stated otherwise, all publications by Mahatma Gandhi have been published by Navajivan Publishing House, Ahmedabad, which was founded during the Mahatma's lifetime.
Gregg, Richard B.: *The Power of Non-Violence*, J. B. Lippincott, Philadelphia, 1934 and Navajivan, Ahmedabad, 1938.

Holmes, John Hayes: *My Gandhi,* Allen and Unwin, London, 1954.

Jack, Homer A. (Editor): *The Wit and Wisdom of Gandhi*, The Beacon Press, Boston, 1951.

Jones, E. Stanley: *Mahatma Gandhi: An Interpretation*, Hodder and Stoughton, London, 1948.

King, Martin Luther, Jr.: *Why We can't Wait!*: Harper and Row, Publishers, New York, 1964.

————: *Stride Towards Freedom*; Harper and Row, N.Y. 1958.

Kaunda, David Kenneth: *Kaunda On Violence*, Sphere Books Ltd, London, 1980.

Kriplani, K. R.: *Tagore, Gandhi and Nehru*, Hind Kitabs, Bombay, 1947.

———— (Editor): *All Men are Brothers*, UNESCO, 1956; Navajivan, 1960.

————: *Gandhi: His Life and Thought*, Ministry of Information and Broadcasting, Government of India, New Delhi, 1970.

Lester, Muriel: *Entertaining Gandhi*, Ivor Nicholson and Watson, London, 1938.

Mahadevan, T. K. and Ramchandran G.: *Gandhi: His Relevance for our Time*, Bharatiya Vidya Bhavan, Bombay, 1967.

————: *Truth and Non-Violence*, Orient Longman, New Delhi, 1970.

Mashruwala, K. G.: *Gandhi and Marx*, Navajivan Publishing House, Ahmedabad, 1951.

Mazumdar, Haridas T.: *Gandhi versus the Empire*, Universal Publishing Co, New York, 1932.

Mazrui, Ali A.: *Political Values and the Educated Class in Africa*, Heinemann Educational Books, London, 1978.

Mehta, Ved: *Mahatma Gandhi and His Apostles*, André Deutsch, London, 1977.

Mirabehn (Madelaine Slade): *Bapu's Letters to Mira*, Navajivan Publishing House, Ahmedabad, 1949.

————: *The Spirit's Pilgrimage*, Longmans Green & Co Ltd, London, 1960.

Morton, Eleanor: *The Women in Gandhi's Life*, Dodd Mead, New York, 1953.

Nag, Kalidas: *Tolstoy and Gandhi*, Pustak Bhandar, Patna, India, 1950.

Nanda, B. R.: *Mahatma Gandhi*, Allen and Unwin, London, and Beacon Press, Boston, 1958.

Nayyar, Sushila: *Kasturba*, Wallingford, Pennsylvania, USA, 1948.

————: *Kasturba: A Personal Reminiscence*, Navajivan, Ahmedabad, 1960.

Nehru, Jawaharlal: *An Autobiography*, John Lane, London, 1936.

————: *The Discovery of India*, Signet Press, Calcutta, 1941.

Parikh, Narhari D.: *Sardar Vallabhbhai Patel*, Navajivan Publishing House, Ahmedabad, 1953.

Payne, Robert: *The Life and Death of Mahatma Gandhi*, The Bodley Head, London, 1969.

Polak, H. S. L.; Brailsford, H. N. and Lord Pethick-Lawrence: *Mahatma Gandhi*, Odhams Press, London, 1931.

Power, Paul F.: *Gandhi on World Affairs*, Public Affairs Press, Washington, 1960.

Prabhu, R.K. (Editor): *Bapu and Children,* Navajivan, Ahmedabad, 1962.

Prasad, Rajendra: *At the Feet of Mahatma Gandhi,* Asia Publishing House, Bombay, 1961.

Pyare Lal: *Mahatma Gandhi: The Early Phase*, Navajivan, Ahmedabad, 1965.

————: *Mahatma Gandhi: The Last Phase* (Vol. I & II), Navajivan, Ahmedabad, 1956, 1958.

Rajagopalachari, C. (Editor): *The Nation's Voice*, Navajivan, Ahmedabad, 1947.

Radhakrishnan, S. (Editor): *Mahatma Gandhi: Essays and Reflections*, Allen and Unwin, London, 1939 and Jaico Publishing House, Bombay, 1956.

———— (Editor): *Mahatma Gandhi: 100 Years*, Gandhi Peace Foundation, New Delhi, 1968.

Rolland, Romain: *Mahatma Gandhi: The Man who Became One With The Universal Being*, Stock, Paris, 1924; Century Co. New York, 1924; Allen and Unwin, London, 1924.

Sheean, Vincent: *Lead Kindly Light*, Random House, New York, 1949 and Cassel & Co Ltd, London, 1949.

Tendulkar, D. G. and Jhaveri, V. K.: *Mahatma*, Volumes 1-8, Times of India Press, Bombay, 1951-54.

Tinker, Hugh: *The Ordeal of Love: C. F. Andrews and India*, O.U.P. Delhi, 1979.

Watson, Francis: *The Trial of Mr. Gandhi*, Macmillan, London, 1969.

————: *Talking of Gandhi*, Longmans, London, 1957.

Index